Brand New

ディスカス

DISCUS

by Hiroshi YAMADA, Fumitoshi MORI, Shuichi FUDE, et al.

This publication is a translation of the book DISCUS, Brand New by Hiroshi Yamada and Fumitoshi Mori. The original book was published in Japanese in 1988. The copyright for the Japanese edition is with the authors and Mr. Keizo Ishizu of Marine Planning in Tokyo.

The TFH edition was up-dated in September, 1991 by Drs. Warren E. Burgess and Herbert R. Axelrod. Additional photographs were added as new varieties of discus have entered the world discus market.

In order to keep the flavor of the book, certain Japanese stylizing was included. In all cases the Japanese characters are accompanied by their translation. The inclusion of Japanese equipment, from the original text, is merely to inform the reader about the kind of equipment available to Japanese hobbyists.

Distributed in the UNITED STATES by T.F.H. Publications, Inc., One T.F.H. Plaza, Neptune City, NJ 07753; in CANADA to the Pet Trade by H & L Pet Supplies Inc., 27 Kingston Crescent, Kitchener, Ontario N2B 2T6; Rolf C. Hagen Ltd., 3225 Sartelon Street, Montreal 382 Quebec; in CANADA to the Book Trade by Macmillan of Canada (A Division of Canada Publishing Corporation), 164 Commander Boulevard, Agincourt, Ontario M1S 3C7; in ENGLAND by T.F.H. Publications, PO Box 15, Waterlooville PO7 6BQ; in AUSTRALIA AND THE SOUTH PACIFIC by T.F.H. (Australia) Pty. Ltd., Box 149, Brookvale 2100 N.S.W., Australia; in NEW ZEALAND by Ross Haines & Son, Ltd., 82 D Elizabeth Knox Place, Panmure, Auckland, New Zealand; in the PHILIPPINES by Bio-Research, 5 Lippay Street, San Lorenzo Village, Makati, Rizal; in SOUTH AFRICA by Multipet Pty. Ltd., P.O. Box 35347, Northway, 4065, South Africa. Published by T.F.H. Publications, Inc. Manufactured in the United States of America by T.F.H. Publications, Inc.

CUSTOMARY U.S. MEASURES AND EQUIVALENTS	METRIC MEASURES AND EQUIVALENTS

LENGTH

1 inch (in)		= 2.54 cm	1 millimeter (mm)		= .0394 in
1 foot (ft)	= 12 in	= .3048 m	1 centimeter (cm)	= 10 mm	= .3937 in
1 yard (yd)	= 3 ft	= .9144 m	1 meter (m)	= 1000 mm	= 1.0936 yd
1 mile (mi)	= 1760 yd	= 1.6093 km	1 kilometer (km)	= 1000 m	= .6214 mi
1 nautical mile	= 1.152 mi	= 1.853 km			

AREA

1 square inch (in²)		= 6.4516 cm²	1 sq centimeter (cm²)	= 100 mm²	= .155 in²
1 square foot (ft²)	= 144 in²	= .093 m²	1 sq meter (m²)	= 10,000 cm²	= 1.196 yd²
1 square yard (yd²)	= 9 ft²	= .8361 m²	1 hectare (ha)	= 10,000 m²	= 2.4711 acres
1 acre	= 4840 yd²	= 4046.86 m²	1 sq kilometer (km²)	= 100 ha	= .3861 mi²
1 square mile(mi²)	= 640 acre	= 2.59 km²			

WEIGHT

1 ounce (oz)	= 437.5 grains	= 28.35 g	1 milligram (mg)		= .0154 grain
1 pound (lb)	= 16 oz	= .4536 kg	1 gram (g)	= 1000 mg	= .0353 oz
1 short ton	= 2000 lb	= .9072 t	1 kilogram (kg)	= 1000 g	= 2.2046 lb
1 long ton	= 2240 lb	= 1.0161 t	1 tonne (t)	= 1000 kg	= 1.1023 short tons
			1 tonne		= .9842 long ton

VOLUME

1 cubic inch (in³)		= 16.387 cm³	1 cubic centimeter (cm³)		= .061 in³
1 cubic foot (ft³)	= 1728 in³	= .028 m³	1 cubic decimeter (dm³)	= 1000 cm³	= .353 ft³
1 cubic yard (yd³)	= 27 ft³	= .7646 m³	1 cubic meter (m³)	= 1000 dm³	= 1.3079 yd³
			1 liter (l)	= 1 dm³	= .2642 gal
1 fluid ounce (fl oz)		= 2.957 cl	1 hectoliter (hl)	= 100 l	= 2.8378 bu
1 liquid pint (pt)	= 16 fl oz	= .4732 l			
1 liquid quart (qt)	= 2 pt	= .946 l			
1 gallon (gal)	= 4 qt	= 3.7853 l			
1 dry pint		= .5506 l			
1 bushel (bu)	= 64 dry pt	= 35.2381 l			

TEMPERATURE

CELSIUS° = 5/9 (F° − 32°)   **FAHRENHEIT° = 9/5 C° + 32°**

CONTENTS

PROFESSIONAL BREEDER'S DISCUS BREEDING METHODS 155

Symphysodon aequifasciata aequifasciata from Lago Tefe.

Contributors to this book (photos, etc.):

Dr. Herbert R. Axelrod

Dr. Clifford Chan

Mr. Chew

Mr. Bernd Degen

Mr. Shuichi Fude

Mr. Gan Kian Boon

Mr. Gan Kian Leng

Mr. Gan Kian Tiong

Mr. Gan (the Elder)

Mr. Kishio Hatai

Mr. Fumitoshi Mori

Dr. Eugene Ng

Mr. Fred Rosenzweig

Mr. Jack Wattley

Mr. Hiroshi Yamada

Mr. Lo Wing Yat

The cover photograph was taken by Mr. Arend van den Nieuwenhuizen.

WILD
DISCUS

BLUE

WILD BLUE DISCUS

Symphysodon aequifasciata haraldi
Geographical distribution: Leticia (Peru), Benjamin Constant, Purus River, and Manacapuru (Brazil).

In step with the increase in the popularity of the discus, the appreciative and critical eye of the discus breeders has become refined.

Royal Blue is quite suitable as the name for this fish. Individuals of this type of discus may have been contributing to the production of improved varieties, such as the "Red Royal Blue" (RRB).

Royal Blue Discus, 13 cm. Thanks to the improved transportation and increased availability of the most colorful individuals, the breeding of these fish has become more and more familiar to hobbyists.

Symphysodon aequifasciata haraldi
A little blue color is seen only near the anal fin base, the dorsal fin base, and the head and the nape. It is not easy to tell this variety from the brown discus. The difference is mainly in the places where the colors develop.

Young Discus, 12 cm. The black band on the dorsal fin shows some abnormality, which may be characteristic of the wild discus. Certainly an original variety can be developed from this fish.

Young Royal Blue Discus. 10 cm.
The red eyes, the stripes along its sides, and its
basic body color make this a wonderfully
balanced individual.

The blue discus, which is often confused with the green discus, has been increasingly imported in recent years. It is widely recognized by its blue stripes on a basic reddish brown background. During the last several years, a lot of considerably high quality fish have been kept by Japanese fanciers. These discus are known as "Royal Blue" discus.

Young Royal Blue Discus, 12 cm.
This species is considered the easiest to breed after the brown discus.

An individual imported from the Peruvian Amazon near Colombia. The fifth bar has been involved in a controversy regarding discus classification.

GREEN

WILD GREEN DISCUS

Symphysodon aequifasciata aequifasciata
Geographic distribution: Lake Tefé, Tefé River, Santarem, Peruvian Amazon.

The basic color is dark yellowish brown or light brown. There is a metallic green-blue color on the head,

Royal Green, 14 cm.
The charm of the Peruvian type, hence its great popularity, is due in part to the many red spots that appea on the sides of the body and the anal fin.

Green Discus, 14 cm.
This green discus adult has the
strong "yellowish" color peculiar to
the green discus. The body shape
is not exactly perfect, but this
happens quite often in the case of
the larger sizes.

Royal Green Discus.
This adult Royal Green discus
exhibits a body color that may
possibly lead to a turquoise discus.
It is particularly attractive around
the base of the anal fin.

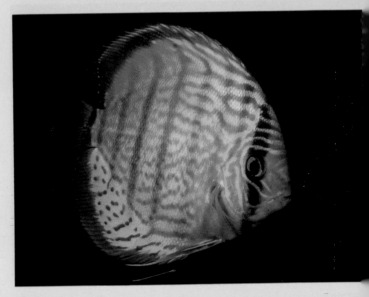

Royal Green Discus, 14 cm.
Blue-green stripes appear
throughout the body. As the fish
grows the stripes become more
distinct.

Royal Green Discus, 12 cm.
Still young, this individual is potentially a winner in view of its green coloration and many red spots.

sides of the body, and around the anal
fin. This is a very pretty original variety
of the discus.

Every year from autumn to spring a
lot of fishes are imported into Japan
from South America and therefore easily

This is the Tefe type green discus which
lacks red spots but has a good, balanced
coloration with the blue-green stripes.

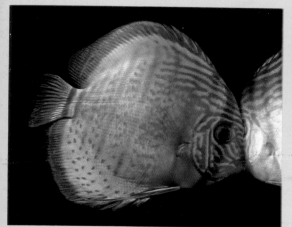

Royal Green, 15 cm.
This male Royal Green discus with breeding
coloration and head down posture can be
compared with the female in the background.

Peruvian Green Discus
This type is normally kept for the improvement of the variety. It is usually paired with the turquoise discus.

obtainable by the Japanese hobbyists. It is the well-known variety known as the turquoise discus that comes from the attractive parents originally collected by Jack Wattley. It is a magnificent sight to see a group of these fish swimming.

Royal Green, 12 cm.
A Tefe green discus of excellent
quality. The attraction here is the
stripes on the head that extend to
the base of the dorsal fin.

Green Discus
This is the commonly seen stress
coloration of the green discus. The
dark bars are quite noticeable as is
the very pale blue-green color of
the sides.

Royal Green Discus, 10-12 cm.
This group of young individuals of
the original variety of Royal Green
discus are rather high quality recent
imports. Breeding of the original
species is being avidly anticipated.

Royal Green Discus. This adult individual has a charm that could not be appreciated from the original variety.

HECKEL

WILD HECKEL BLUE DISCUS

Symphysodon discus var.
Geographical distribution: Rio Negro, Rio Trombetas, Rio Madeira (Abacaxis).

This species was originally described in 1840 by Dr. J. Heckel. The fifth dark bar is broad and referred to as the "Heckel" band. Needless to say, this Heckel band makes it relatively easy to

A pair of Heckel Discus, 14cm. Breeding Heckel discus has been attracting a great deal of discus fans. This is a rather realistic dream that could readily come true.

Heckel Discus.
The fifth dark band in the Heckel discus becomes indistinct when the fish is in good condition and in breeding color. It is therefore recommended that they be kept alone—without any other types of discus.

Heckel Discus.
This is the most delicate of the discus. It can be "tamed," however, with proper daily maintenance.

Heckel Discus.
The numbers imported yearly has been fairly constant. The 10-12cm young fish are more hardy and easier to keep.

Heckel Blue Discus, 19 cm.
A young Heckel Blue discus only a few days after having been
imported.

A complete decorative layout with gravel, plants, driftwood, etc.,
can be enjoyed fully with this species. Generally such a layout is
taboo when keeping the improved varieties. The blue coloration in
this individual is brilliant.

distinguish from the others. A great deal
of effort has been expended crossing
this fish with the turquoise (RRB) as
well as within its own species.

20

Every year, from winter to early spring, great numbers of this discus are imported together with cardinal tetras and rummy-nose tetras from South America.

A pair of Heckel Blue discus exhibiting shining narrow blue stripes. When keeping several of them pairing behavior can frequently be observed.

BROWN

WILD BROWN DISCUS

Symphysodon aequifasciata axelrodi
Geographical distribution: Around Belem, Rio Urubu, to near Manaus.

The brown discus is the most popular of the original subspecies in the history of discus-keeping. It appears to the hobbyist as the "king of tropical fishes." Its basic coloration is yellowish to reddish brown. More than 90% of the

Brown Discus.
Perfect brown discus adult, collected from the natural habitat. It has a strong yellowish basic coloration.

Brown Discus, 15 cm.
This adult male has a rather gray
ground color. The breeding, like
that of the green and the blue
discus, requires more technique
than those bred in Hong Kong.

Brown Discus.
Seeing this fish, you can be
encouraged to believe that tomato-
red discus live in the Amazon
system.

The classification of discus is far
from perfect. A lot of intermediates
between the different subspecies
(ex. *aequifasciata* and *axelrodi*) can
be seen.

Brown Discus, 14 cm male.
The wonderful overall proportions, the red eye,
and the refined basic coloration cannot be trifled
with even though this is a brown discus.

Brown Discus.
Young brown discus collected near Belem. The basic reddish brown color is really worth appreciating.

Brown Discus.
This is a yellow variation of the brown discus known as the "golden" discus. The overall milky white color of the body has intensified as it grew.

Brown Discus.
Brown discus are raised in Thailand and Singapore. Some feed their discus prawn eggs, which enhances their color.

fish seen today in Japan are those bred in Hong Kong and Southeast Asian countries. Very few are from the Amazon system, where their coloration is quite unique and could not be missed. They are the best for discus beginners.

This adult brown discus was bred in Hong Kong. The blue stripes can be seen on the head and anal fin. They are prettier than those seen in the natural habitat.

Hong Kong is quite a distance from the Amazon, but the discus raised there are quite domesticated due to the many years of artificial breeding.

ARTIFICIAL
VARIETY

TURQUOISE

TURQUOISE DISCUS

The turquoise discus was produced by Mr. Jack Wattley. The second generation of this discus has been called the "German" Turquoise and the following varieties of this type have been produced: Cobalt Blue, Cobalt Flash, Red, and Brilliant. These masterpieces have also been imported

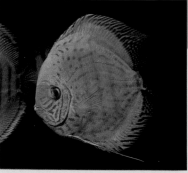

Adult German Cobalt Blue Discus.

Cobalt Blue Turquoise.
The body color of this adult is really so good it is worthy enough to be called a turquoise green. The stripes always attract the researcher's interest.

Green Turquoise.
The blue pattern on the head of this male fish is peculiar—it implies "strength."

Adult Female German "Wattley."
The proportions, the redness of the eyes, and the beautiful basic blue coloration all appeal to the viewer.

Green Metallic Cobalt, 9 cm.
The natural nobility is seen in the cobalt variety even in this young fish.

into Japan and have become the leading turquoise kept today. On the other hand, about 200 professional turquoise discus breeders in Germany still produce new and improved types. These will be our targets in the future. During these past few years, turquoise discus have also been produced in Hong Kong and Southeast Asian countries and the imports from these areas into Japan have been increasing.

Adult German Cobalt Blue Turquoise. The basic color is reddish brown. The blue color will spread, and with a good body shape and long fins, some will be qualified to be called "super good" fish.

ARTIFICIAL VARIETY

[top left]
German "Wattley"
Discus, 10 cm.
The large fins and
the body lacking
any deformations
in its shape make
the fish appear
larger than its
actual size. This
is a beautiful fish.

[top right]
German Cobalt
Blue Turquoise
Discus.

[second row left]
Adult Male
German Cobalt
Blue Turquoise.
The rather pale
blue color over
the entire body is
very elegant and
impressive.

[second row right]
Young German
Cobalt Blue
Turquoise.
Nothing more
could be wished
for when the blue
color appears in
such intensity in
7-10 cm fish.

[third row left]
Adult German
Cobalt Blue
Turquoise.
Sooner or later
the blue color will
completely cover
every part of the
body.

[third row right]
German Cobalt
Blue Turquoise
Discus.
This fish appears
a bit exhausted. It
has just finished
spawning. We
would like to
challenge anyone
to breed such
good fish as this.

[bottom row left]
Adult Male
German
"Wattley," 16 cm.
Keeping German
Turquoise discus
is somewhat
difficult because
of its sensitivity to
environmental
conditions.

[bottom row right]
German Cobalt
Blue Discus.
Among young fish
imported under
this name are
found many with
this pattern of
stripes.

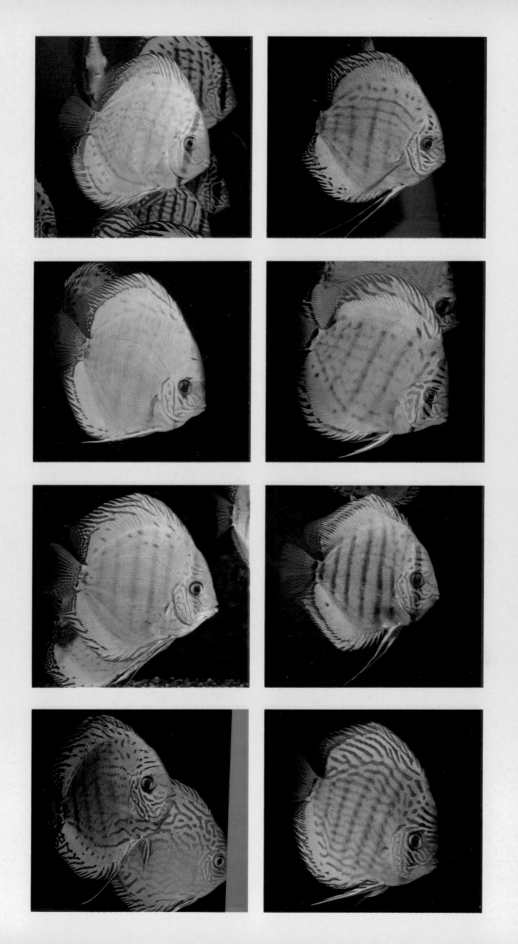

German Brilliant Turquoise, 10 cm. The dark blue color on the dorsal and anal fin bases makes us well aware of the potential beauty that will develop later.

Adult German "Wattley." The body color of many German turquoise discus becomes more intense after reaching a size of 12 cm.

Adult German Cobalt Flash
Turquoise.
This fish exhibits the typical basic
color.

Adult German "Wattley."
This fish shows its dark bars
because of stress. This kind of fish,
as it grows, will change to a well
balanced appearance.

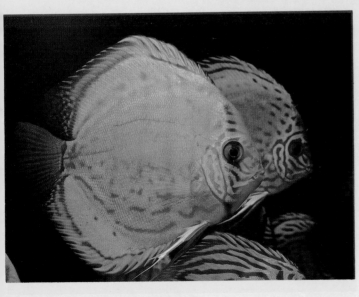

Young German Cobalt Flash
Turquoise.
Fish of about 10 cm size, only
occasionally imported, have almost
all a high quality of beauty.

German Cobalt Blue Turquoise.
The turquoise green color has spread
widely over the entire body of
outstanding proportions.

German Bred Turquoise of "Stripe" Red Strain.
This is insufficient in view of the phenotype but good because of its being voluminous.

German Cobalt Flash Turquoise, 10 cm young.
The blue color is well distributed as expected.

German "Wattley", 12 cm adult.
The deep turquoise green contrasts well with the basic color of yellowish brown. The combination makes this fish very interesting.

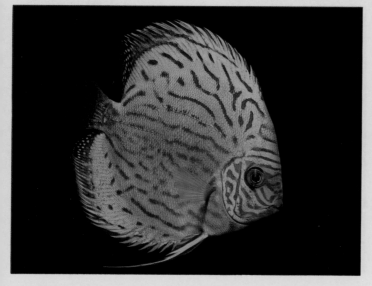

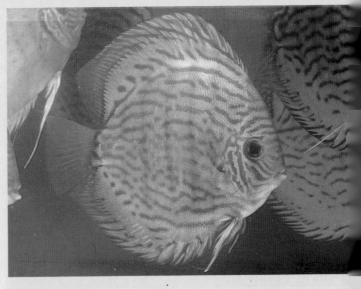

Hong Kong breeder Mr. S. Yuen keeps this female fish for breeding. Frozen food with marine shrimp as its main ingredient was fed in quantity along with live worms.

"Stripe" Turquoise line, 14 cm. At the peak of development of the blue stripes the fish is similar to the original species and increases its appeal.

Hong Kong Highfin "Wattley," 9 cm young fish. Though these fish are Hong Kong bred, they may often be F_1 of German Turquoise discus as there is not very much difference between them.

German Red Turquoise.
The color is beautifully balanced and attractive, showing its basic color, red. This is different from the RRB.

F₁ Generation from turquoise and RRB Parents.
The turquoise blood line is seen in its dorsal and anal fins.

A female of Degen's famous "Red Scribbled" discus. The fish has an excellent body shape and size.

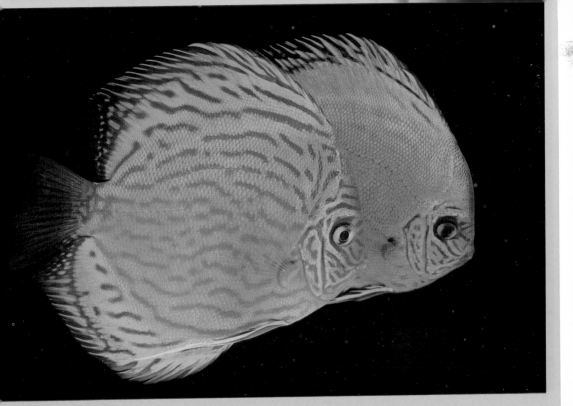

Adult Male Highfin "Wattley," 15 cm.
This adult was raised from fry of 5 cm. They have been raised to quite wonderful specimens.

Adult Male Highfin "Wattley," 7 cm.
If these would be imported in quantity, 5 to 6 individuals of this fish would be recommended to be purchased without any hesitation.

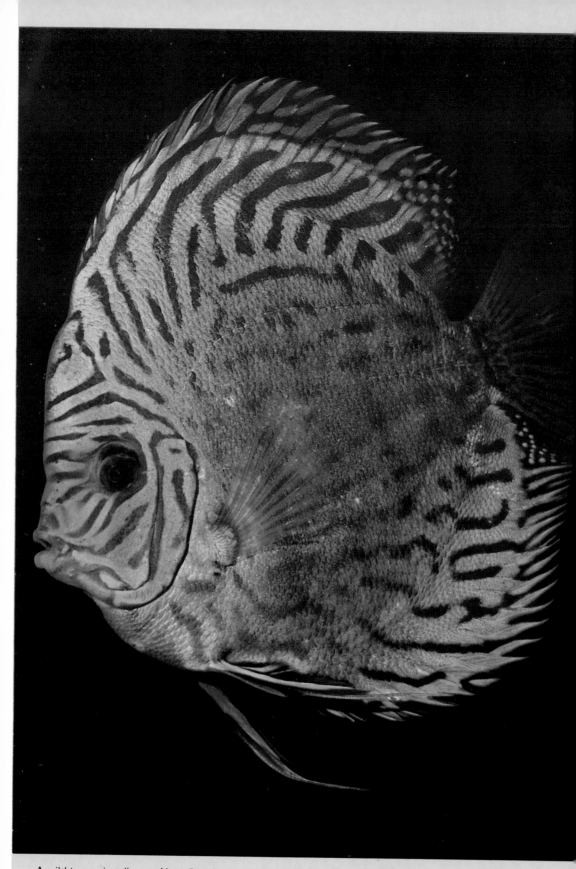

A wild turquoise discus. Note the absence of the characteristic red eyes.

A beautifully shaped cobalt blue discus with brilliant colors.

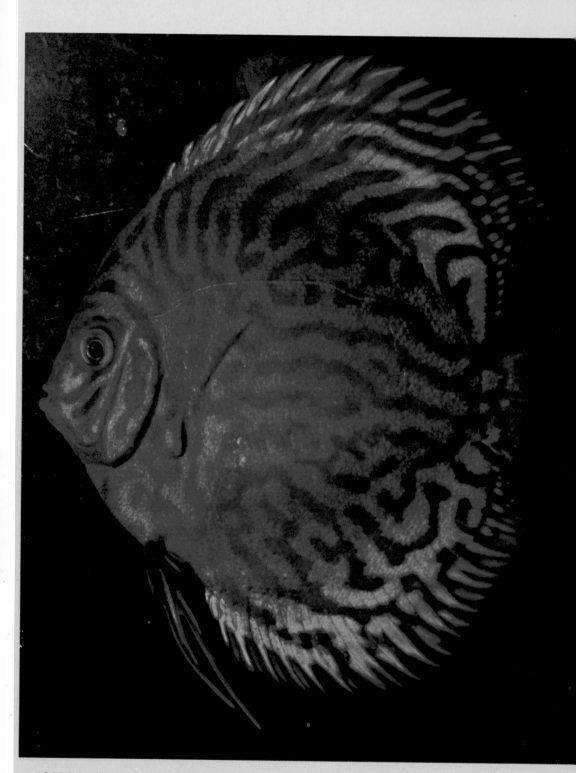

A high-bodied turquoise discus with a reddish brown background color.

A brilliant turquoise discus with an interesting pattern.

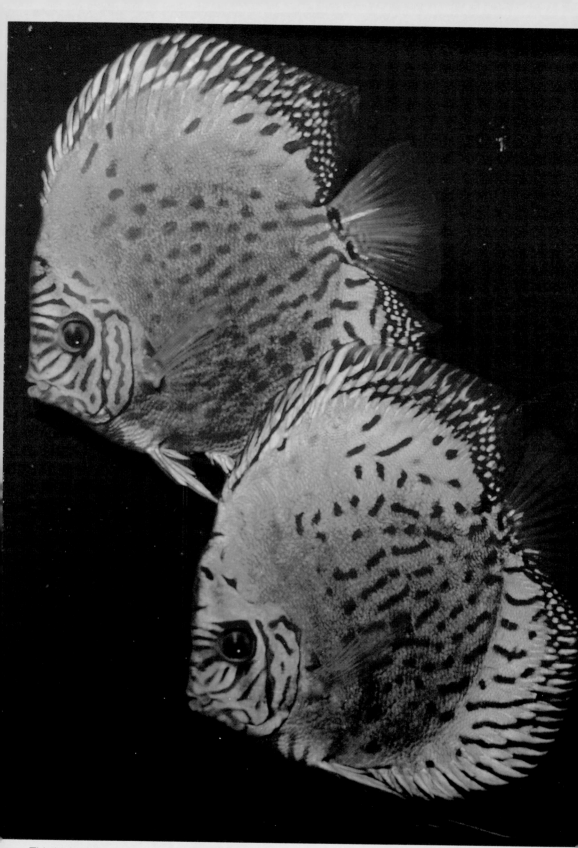

This high-bodied pair won top prize at Singapore's AQUARAMA '89. They were obtained from cobalt and turquoise parents.

Gan Khian Tiong's turquoise discus. Some faint vertical bars are evident.

Although quite young, this turquoise has a good body shape.

The pattern exhibited by this pair of turquoise discus is generally referred to as "scribbled."

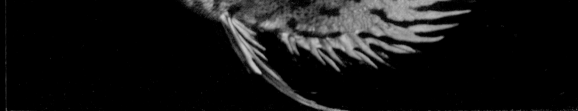

This young adult turquoise discus shows good body shape along with the typical Gan striations.

Highfin Cobalt Blue Turquoise.
A high and well balanced body with beautiful
dorsal and anal fins is seen.

Turquoise discus of the "Stripe" line, 12 cm.
The overall volume of the body is still
insufficient, but the body is well balanced
with good shape, stripes, and fins.

Young Highfin "Wattley," 12 cm.
This fish has the bright blue color over the
whole body. The color will gradually become
darker.

Young Highfin "Wattley," 12 cm.
The basic coloration appears spotted. This
pattern of remaining spots assures that the
blue color will spread well later.

Hong Kong Highfin "Wattley."
An adult female with the blue color
appearing over the whole body. This fish will
grow up to be a good mother for selective
breeding.

Hong Kong "Wattley" Turquoise, 8 cm.
The stripes on this fish are irregular. It looks
interesting but not quite satisfactory.

Adult Male Highfin Cobalt Blue.
Being sexually excited, the male begins
to secrete mucus from his body surface.
This fish looks quite strong as a breeding
parent.

Giant Red Male. This male is protecting eggs in the spawning tank of Mr. Yat Sunny. If this color strain could remain fixed its popularity would rapidly rise.

A pair of High-body Giant Turquoise, the great masterpiece of Mr. Yat Sunny. Nothing more could be required from these fish in view of the intensity of the blue color and the body shape, which are really superior.

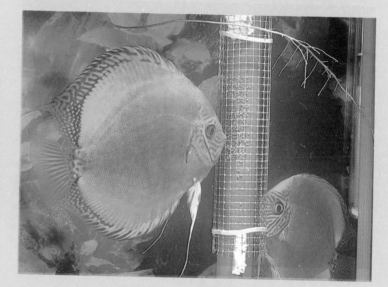

Highfin Cobalt Blue Turquoise. The mother fish originally produced by Mr. Yat Sunny. We are surprised with his production and enthusiastic research endeavors.

A male parent of a dark blue turquoise discus with a very colorful body and quite a number of the fry crowded around him.

A group of baby turquoise discus swimming in Mr. S. Yuen's stock tank. With daily water changes of 1/3 to 1/2, 200-300 individuals can be accommodated in his 90 cm tank.

15 cm adult male. Body shape, stripes, redness of the eye—all of these points are excellent. This is a product of Mr. S. Yuen. This type has been the most produced, among others, which are at the same time the most impressive.

Adult male. Broad stripes spread throughout the sides of the body. Mr. S. Yuen has successfully bred them by waiting for a pair to form naturally, keeping 2 males and 1 female fish.

The shape and color could not be considered better than others, but this female is a very good parent with regard to the care of the young. It is said that this type has stronger breeding capabilities.

An excellent turquoise of the "Stripe" line. This one seems just to correspond to the ideal of "13 stripes." Surprisingly, it has been learned that the fish are fed only with live bloodworms.

A 10 cm "Fude Turquoise" with a unique red being its base color, which is developed from the carotene in its diet of marine shrimp.

A 12 cm "Fude Turquoise." The body is high, the head round, and the respective fins are all well balanced, which may be characteristic to this group of fish.

Young "Fude Turquoise," 10-12 cm. Turquoise blue coloring appears all over the body. If the body should be rounder and thicker, it would be perfect.

3-4 cm "Fude Turquoise." The recent tendency is to expect from this group of fish more quality than quantity.

Baby "Fude Turquoise" accommodated in a 60 cm tank have instantly eaten the offered frozen bloodworms. The quality of these baby fish is very high.

A 15 cm "Matsukawaya Turquoise" of the
"Stripe" line. The high body, large dorsal and
anal fins, and long pelvic fins are excellent.

"Matsukawaya Turquoise" with a hint of Wattley
pattern. The body is over 15 cm and has a
unique base color formation on the body.

Adult male "Matsukawaya Turquoise."
A year and a half old with such great dignity. Attention is to be paid to the swell of the head and the filamen
on the soft edge of the dorsal fin.

Adult female
"Matsukawaya Turquoise."
The blue color does not fail
to spread over the body.
The color intensity is also
quite good.

All Matsukawaya
Turquoise fish are like this.
The Japanese breeder's
common sense is to try
and retain a high standard
of fish quality.

WATTLEY

WATTLEY VARIETIES

The history of the turquoise discus is the same as that of the Wattley discus. Thousands of discus have been collected in the Jurua River, a tributary of the Amazon system, among which seven *S. aequifasciata* were found that are the origin of the turquoise discus kept today

This is one of the Jack Wattley discus that grows to a 12 cm adult size. The reason for the reddish basic color is because of the food it eats and not heredity.

An adult Wattley discus that was introduced by Mr. Jack Wattley when he visited Japan.

This Jack Wattley female discus shows perfect form.

Adult fish of Jack Wattley's third strain, which has been kept from the time it was a baby. This fish is a little too slim, which may be influenced by the artificial spawning. A little more bulk could be desired.

Young fish of J. Wattley's third strain whose blue color covers so much of the entire body that the base coloration appears somewhat irregular.

Adult fish with brilliant blue-green broad stripes, which is of J. Wattley's third strain. The importation of fish over 10 cm in size has been long awaited.

An 8-month old Schmidt-Focke cross from a royal turquoise and a Manacapuru discus.

by so many worldwide fanciers. Turquoise is the name of a blue Turkish stone. Seventeen generations of turquoise discus have been bred so far as of today, and the brilliancy of the blue color has still been maintained. The variety inherited the excellent fish blood of German Turquoise being produced, while the characteristics of the pure lineage of turquoise has been successfully kept. The preservation and improvement of the third family line and Highfin/Full Body family line are to be carefully observed as it requires expert breeding technique.

The offspring of the turquoise discus bred by Mr. Jack Wattley after it was brought over from Germany were called Dutch Turquoise and have produced many different varieties. These are Cobalt Blue, Cobalt Flake, Red Brilliant, etc. All of these different kinds of varieties are masterpieces and are imported into Japan one by one. They are the main discus imported today.

But the 200 breeders in Japan are still working to improve the species and breeding new strains. It will be our main purpose in the future. For the last few years the turquoise discus has been bred and imported into Japan from Hong Kong and Southeast Asia and continues to increase.

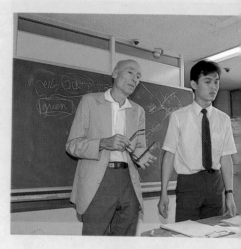

Jack Wattley giving a lecture on discus at Chiba, Japan.

Jack Wattley posing with Mitsuo in Hirose, Japan.

Another Wattley high-fin with an intense solid turquoise color.

RED ROYAL BLUE

"Color discus," which is the origin of Red Royal Blue (RRB) discus, was first introduced as an artificially improved variety according to the history of Japanese discus breeding. In the Southeast Asian countries, especially in Bangkok, the improvement was performed on the *S. aequifasciata* line, and the blue stripes covering the entire body sides were obtained.

Comparatively speaking, these stripes

A 14 cm RRB showing its splendid blue stripes.

A female RRB with broad blue stripes.

have become recently stable. Due to the feeding of marine shrimp and lobster eggs with the red pigment temporarily transferred to the discus, the fish look vividly brilliant over the entire body. This intensive appealing feature will keep this fish as one of the two leaders, along with the turquoise.

A young breeding female of Degen's "Red Royal." The straight red lines are the result of careful selection.

69

Degen's newest cross is this "Red Rio Purus." The adult fish have a very strong red color.

Bernd Degen travels far and wide to find excellent discus specimens for breeding as well as to sell his own strains. Here he is visiting a fish exporter in Taiwan.

Quite a number of RRB discus have been imported every week. Being recently more reasonably priced, the purchase of several individuals at a time has not been difficult.

A young 12 cm RRB discus that was reared from a size of 3 cm with frozen bloodworms and live daphnia only. The water quality maintenance procedures must have been well kept.

Adult RRB discus whose pattern around the dorsal and anal fins is interestingly unique. The peculiar beauty could be maintained further if the reddish tint in the basic body color could possibly be retained with the help of certain devised foods.

A magnificent body shape, worthy of its name "Royal." This fish has been reared in Bangkok and fully appreciated in every respect by the Bangkok breeders.

Adult RRB discus that is overall indistinctly blue. This class of RRB discus is plentifully stocked by Bangkok breeders.

The fifth dark color bar on the body appears a little broader than the others. This kind of RRB discus has been known for quite a while.

Always strikingly pretty are a group of RRB babies. Good rearing depends entirely on the breeder's dedication and good selective appreciation capability.

"Marine Blue"—a new type of RRB discus that young Bangkok breeders produced by crossing German Turquoise with RRB.

Shirase Thunder Flash, male, where the blue color is developing over its entire body. The thick body is well qualified to be an 'adult male.'

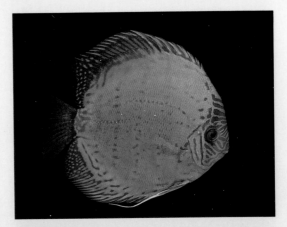

A group of 6 cm Thunder Flash discus. With no color enhancing treatment having been made, the blue color has not yet developed but is very promising in the near future.

A Thunder Flash adult female, raised from its baby stage with its fixation rate being very high. The good daily regular maintenance will make this a considerably attractive fish.

A Thunder Flash female of the "Stripe" line. Beautiful stripes extend from the head to the caudal fin. This may be the supreme accomplishment among the Japanese.

This is the F₁ produced by Mr. Awajiya, Osaka, between RRB female and original Royal Green discus. The male blood lineage appears strongly in the ventral area.

A young Turquoise "Marine Blue." The roundness of the body and the size of the fins having been supplemented by German Turquoise discus blood, they are quite improved.

A young RRB discus, about 6 cm long. The popular size of the imported individuals is 3-4 cm. Occasionally, this size is also imported. The bigger it is, the easier it is to rear further.

A RRB adult, with the stripes appearing wonderfully on the side of the body. The RRB discus had been bred more in quantity than for quality. It has been, however, greatly improved as can be seen by the beauty of this fish.

A RRB discus adult with high form beautiful body shape. Continuous feeding of ample carotene contained in the food must be the prerequisite for keeping the red color.

This is a RRB discus imported from Singapore. This is sometimes called a Heckel discus even though it has no Heckel blood.

A RRB adult discus of the "Full Body" Line. The difference between it and the turquoise is only whether or not it was once crossed with turquoise discus.

BREEDING

A female turquoise discus putting 10-20 eggs on the substrate in a row, row by row. Her body color also begins to intensify.

A pair of turquoise discus cleaning a spawning cone. This action starts 1-3 hours before the spawning, when the pair begins to harmoniously work well together.

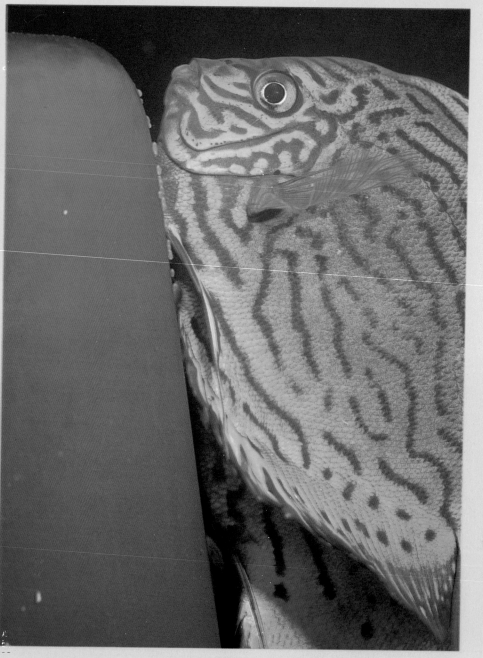

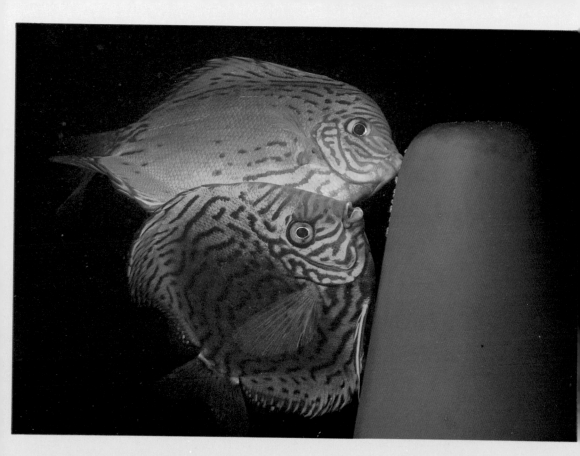

Egg-laying by the female and fertilization of the eggs by the male proceed alternatively row by row.

The male fertilizing the eggs that have been deposited by the female. In case his sperm is lacking in quantity, strong water currents around the spawning cone should be banned during this action.

After spawning, it would be better if the spawning cone is covered by a net in case the parents should suddenly start fighting. It is also an effective way to observe the results (percentage of fertilized eggs, number of eggs, etc.) of the first spawning.

In 1988 Mr. Awajiya succeeded in crossbreeding a female turquoise discus with a male Heckel Blue discus.

A female turquoise discus of the
"Stripe" variety, with her fry feeding
on the "milk." This is nearly to the
point where it can be called a
successful spawning.

Turquoise discus babies two weeks
old. It is recommended that time be
taken to wean them from feeding
from the parents' mucus to brine
shrimp larvae.

Breeding of Brown Discus

As regards discus breeding, a lot of people have employed many data of the environmental preparation and water quality preservation method. Thanks to them, it is elucidated as of today that breeding could be successful only if the conditions would be in order. If you can get a pair out of your painstakingly raised discus and their spawning takes

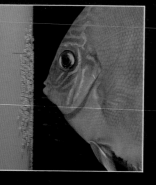

1 Brown discus, the common name "red" applied after feeding with marine shrimp eggs.

4 Hatching begins 60 hours after spawning at a water temperature of 28 C (82 F). About 170 fry hatched out of about 300 eggs.

2 Spawning accomplished at a water depth of 25 cm.

3 The parent fish fans away any "dust" on eggs with its pectoral fins.

 The fry soon after hatching. The parents relocate some of them in order to make more room.

The fry 30 hours after hatching. Their eyes are now gradually forming and their tails start to swing continuously.

The fry 60 hours after spawning. Bunches of 4-10 fry may become stuck together as the organs of attachment on their heads have become intertwined. At this point they are ready to move into their free-swimming period.

place immediately in front of you, it must be nothing else than a charming moment of discus keeping.

You can balance feeding and water quality control, taking into consideration water temperature, pH value, hardness, etc., and taking care of the eggs and fry with more affection than their own parents. The breeding success must be enjoyed only after all the above have been performed.

Let's learn from the accompanying photos all about successful discus breeding as our final target.

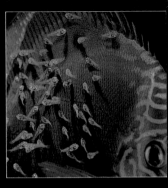

Six days after hatching. The fry are getting used to eating baby brine shrimp at the same time as the discus milk. For good growth they have to be fed five to six times a day.

The total amount of milk ingested from their parents' sides becoming greater as they grow, the fry move busily every minute or two from their mother to their father and vice versa.

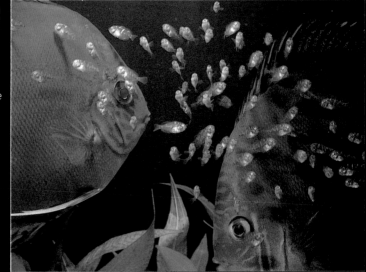

The parents' body surfaces are getting rather coarse. The fry are starting to become independent from the parents, coming toward the aquarist when he approaches, expecting brine shrimp larvae to be fed.

cm long. 19 days after initial feeding
parents' body surfaces. At this point
problem if they are taken from their
d kept separate. This scene would
ring even if you would endlessly
hem.

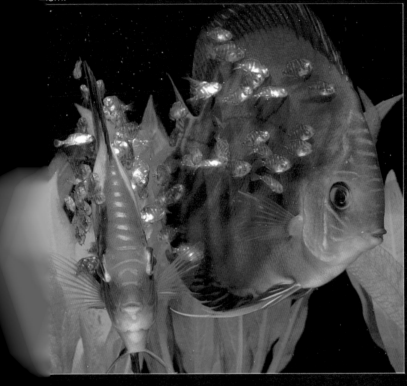

DISEASES OF DISCUS AND THEIR CURES

BY KISHIO HATAI

As long as there are living creatures, certainly there will be death. Discus are no exception. If your discus dies because of old age we can accept it, but if the fish dies due to sickness or accident, we feel very bad about it afterward. Some will certainly feel like giving up raising discus. Everyone who tries to keep and raise discus will have this problem at least once.

Discus are especially sensitive regarding the different circumstances they face in spite of the fact that they were raised in a stable environment for a long time. They can contract diseases by changing their body conditions.

On the other hand, the reasons why there are many discus lovers is not only because of their elegance, but also because of the satisfaction of raising and breeding fish that are difficult for other hobbyists to keep.

In many cases where discus have died, there are various conditions wherein science has not been able to determine the cause(s). Most of the time there are enlightening discussions and conclusions concerning the cause of death through experience or examination, but you cannot plan on it happening every time. It is very difficult for the average person to know the reason for the death of a fish because they would have to research it using a microscope to see if there are any parasites, a process involving separation, cultivation, permanent fixing, and a system to identify diseases along with visual inspection.

At the present time, in our division office, we are using scientific methods to get to the heart of diseases. I am going to introduce you to the reasons diseases occur and suggest countermeasures for you to take. At the same time I want to make a comment about cautions on raising and caring for discus and suggest easy ways to find out what diseases your discus may have—the symptoms of which are already clear to you. Therefore, we need to research the causes before trying to find a cure. When the causes come clear, you can cure them.

It is columnaris disease if your fish is grayish white in color or giving off viscous fluids from the body. When you find small white spots, it will be white spot disease.

Discus sometimes breathe faster than usual. They open and shut the mouth and gill openings very fast. If your oxygen supply is good, it means they have *Chilodonella*, a type of protozoan, on their gills.

It is possible that they have columnaris disease when they lose appetite (change the food or check the water conditions) or rub themselves on the water plants or decorations. It is also possible that there is some kind of parasite or some kind of pathogenic organism in the aquarium. Try inspecting the quality of the water, etc.

THE EARLY DETECTION OF DISEASES

1. Gradual or sudden loss of appetite.
2. Odd swimming behavior or remaining quietly in the corner of the aquarium.
3. Rubbing their bodies on something.
4. Body color changes to abnormal colors.
5. There are abnormal body conditions like bleeding, secretion of viscous fluids, etc.

We can then recognize the early symptoms of the disease or the early conditions of the illness. But if we miss these symptoms or ignore them, the disease will most likely become worse. We will probably kill a fish that could have been cured. Early detection is extremely important.

Since all the reasons for discus diseases are not clear, there are some diseases we cannot cure. Therefore it is important that you have the knowledge to distinguish them.

Typical external appearance of some dead or dying diseased discus. Early detection is extremely important. **1.** The body is quite thin and the dorsal fin is heavily eroded. The skin may be affected by various bacilli, such as *Flexibacter columnaris* or *Aeromonas* sp. **2.** The caudal fin has partially disintegrated and the rear half of the body is eroded and changed to a white color where it is covered by cotton-like hyphae. It is affected by fungus (water mold) disease. **3.** Although appearing somewhat normal, this discus is obviously malnourished and very skinny. Possibly it suffers from some nutritional disorder or problems in the internal organs. It may be affected by nematodes or flagellates (parasites). **4.** If the body becomes blackish and the fish has difficulty breathing, it may be infected by *Chilodonella* or other disease.

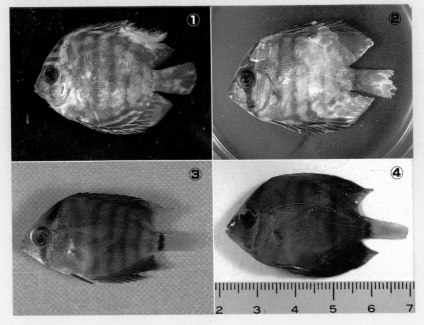

To prevent the development or spread of the disease, first of all you must know the reason why it was able to get a foothold on the fish.

Overfeeding is not the only reason for bad digestion. Another reason is because of a pathogenic organism caused by dirty water from a picky eater.

Feeding should fill 80% of the fish's stomach regularly each day. You should not feed the fish at night because the food will rot quickly by virtue of the increased quantity of oxygen in the water.

It is important to wash live food in enough water to clean it thoroughly before you feed it to your fish. If you do not do it, this can cause white spot disease or germs. You have to realize that the live foods might have had pathogenic organisms on them when they were purchased.

Sometimes, when you put discus in an aquarium with other fishes, they contract some disease from the other fishes within a few days. This will tell you that the fish in the aquarium that looked healthy carried the disease. You better watch the fish and keep them in a separate aquarium for a few days.

Maintaining the proper raising density is important in order to prevent the growth of disease. If the raising density is high, the fish are in a stressful condition and this will make them sick easily. Also, high raising density causes rubbing and a shortage of oxygen, changing the water quality. The fish will also have reason to get sick when you chase them with a net when you change the water in order to move them to another aquarium with different water quality.

I have written down the simple causes of diseases. Theoretically, if you can control the aquarium management you are supposed to be able to prevent diseases. But discus will get sick even if you believe that you are raising them carefully. This tells you that the discus are very sensitive. Therefore, if you suspect that they are sick, you should take countermeasures right away.

ABNORMAL APPEARANCE OR BEHAVIOR

When some kinds of unusual conditions are present in the aquarium, in many cases the body of the discus will change to a darker color. Although a dark body color is a danger sign, there are many reasons for the change of body color, and it is impossible to tell the disease from the dark color.

The body will also turn dark when there is a change of water quality. They are especially sensitive to pH changes, improper feeding, stress, fighting between members of the same species, larger fish picking on smaller ones, and disease.

DISSECTION AS A MEANS FOR DETERMINING CAUSE OF DISEASE

When a discus dies it is important to conduct an autopsy as soon as possible before the body is disposed of. By doing this, identification of the probable cause of death, which was not clearly discernible by external appearance, will be possible. For this reason, you must be familiar with the names of the internal organs of the fish as seen in the accompanying illustrations.

If the cause of death was not identified from external examination, first check the gills. A discus can easily die from respiratory problems when there is an injury or damage to the respiratory organs. When observing the gills, you will be able to see if the discus was suffering from anemia by checking its color. If there is any discoloration, columnaris disease can be suspected. If there are any small white spots, white spot disease can be suspected. If there

Anatomical chart of discus.

1. KIDNEY	2. SWIM BLADDER
3. PRONEPHROS	4. HEART
5. LIVER	6. GENITAL TUBE
7. STOMACH	8. INTESTINE

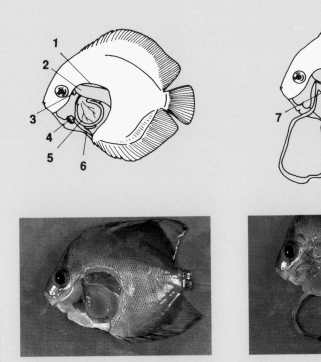

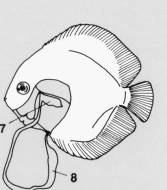

is any abnormal mucus secretion, *Chilodonella* or gill fluke disease can be suspected.

When observing the internal organs, anemia can be checked the same way—by looking at the color. If bleeding spots or red spots appear on all parts of the organs and there is swelling of the spleen, the bacterial disease caused by *Aeromonas* can be suspected.

MICROSCOPIC EXAMINATION TO DETERMINE CAUSES OF DISEASES

If the disease is related to pathogenic organisms, a naked-eye study will not be sufficient. The use of a microscope with an enlargement capacity of 400X will be necessary, making visible the variety of pathogenic organisms on the infected parts of the body and gills. Although different kinds of pathogenic organisms will be visible, you must be able to recognize the most prominent and to apply adequate treatment.

An epithelioma (epidermal cystic tumor) affecting the gills of a fish. Tissue photograph (H & E stained, 40X).

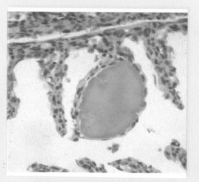

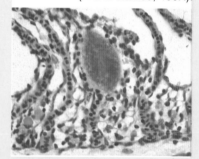

Above; An epithelioma. Tissue photograph (H & E stained, 400X). Below; Adhesion of the gill cells is seen surrounding the epithelioma. Tissue photograph (H & E stained, 400X).

COMMON DISEASES

1. EPITHELIOCYSTIS DISEASE

This was first recorded by Hoffman, et al. (1969) as a chronic disease of bluegills and it was only reported after its discovery in other fishes. Its distribution is practically worldwide, and because it is found in marine fishes, brackish water fishes, and freshwater fishes, it is thought to have little preference in hosts.

The disease is caused by an epidermal cystic tumor, ranging from 10 to more than 100 microns in size, which forms in large numbers on the gills and can be seen with the naked eye

94

(appearing as white cyst-like spots). There is still much that is not known about the affect or damage to the fish, but once the epidermal cystic tumor forms on the gills, it can cause a thickening of the skin layer, a deformation or conglutination (hyperplasia). Therefore, when many epidermal cystic tumors form on the gills, the fish is very likely to have breathing difficulties. It is also possible that a secondary disease may be contracted atop the primary one. Furthermore, depending upon changes in the environment (such as water quality) and handling, the fish will be less resistant to stress.

SYMPTOMS

The infected fish usually will not show any symptoms although this depends upon the degree of infection. The only change will be that the fish will turn blackish in color. There won't even be a change in its swimming pattern.

In the example given here, the epidermal cystic tumor was scattered over the gills, so we assumed much of the body was not affected. But we found that part of the gill's outer layer was conglutinated or stuck together. Look for small white spots if checking with the naked eye.

CAUSE

The cystic tumor is an enlarged epidermal cell or a mucous cell and the pathogen found within is of 0.3 to 2 microns in size. These are thought to be a kind of rickettsia based on their shape and way of staining.

COUNTER-MEASURES

None known. So far, since there haven't been any predominant cases of the disease even in tropical fishes, there hasn't been any need for preventive measures. However, since there is a chance of a secondary disease, it is necessary to take measures against the latter one.

2. COLUMNARIS DISEASE

This is a typical bacterial disease frequently found in freshwater fishes living in warm waters. Tropical fishes kept in warmer water temperatures are especially susceptible to this disease. The infected fish may have the ends of its fins deteriorated or its lips inflamed. The gills may be partially decayed, but this will not be known until the gill cover has been opened. From characteristics such as these, the disease is generally known as fin rot, tail rot, or gill rot.

SYMPTOMS

The parts most susceptible to columnaris are the fins as well as the gills. The part infected will deteriorate or decay. When looking closely at the infected area, it may appear to have yellow things stuck to it.

The causative bacteria, classified in the family of mucous bacteria, has the characteristic of secreting mucus, making it look as if there's a cloudiness around the infected area when viewed with the naked eye. When magnified, a colony of cylindrically-shaped bacteria can be seen and many long bacilli are found around it. Therefore, the diagnosis of the disease is relatively easy.

CAUSE

Caused by *Flexibacter columnaris*, a species of gliding bacteria. It is a gram-negative long bacillus that glides or moves by flexion, having no flagella. Generally known as a columnaris bacterium.

COUNTER-MEASURES

The disease can be treated with a medication sold under the name of Parazan or Green F Gold. Adding a small amount of salt to

Flexibacter columnaris colony, columnar stacks of bacterial cells, formed on diseased surface. Microphotograph (200X).

the medication is helpful. However, if the disease is in its terminal stage, no treatment will be useful. Early detection and early treatment are important.

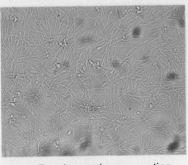

Many *F. columnaris* propagating around diseased part. Microphotograph (1000X).

3. AEROMONAS

This disease is contracted through an abrasion on the skin. If the *Aeromonas* bacterium exists in the aquarium, it will be contracted through this abrasion and spread through the entire body, finally causing blood poisoning or septicemia, killing the fish. The bacterium is more active in lower temperatures than in warmer. Therefore, if water temperature is kept around 30°C, there is less chance for the disease to occur.

SYMPTOMS

Part or most of the skin may look abraded, showing congestion or rubefaction. The infected fish will weaken rapidly and will die as soon as symptoms start to show.

CAUSE

Caused by *Aeromonas hydrophila*. This is a gram-negative short bacillus that swims with its only flagellum. Many short bacilli will be visible when the inspected area is observed.

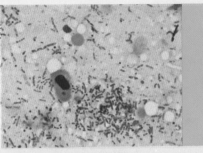

A smear of diseased skin.
(Giemsa stain, 1000X).

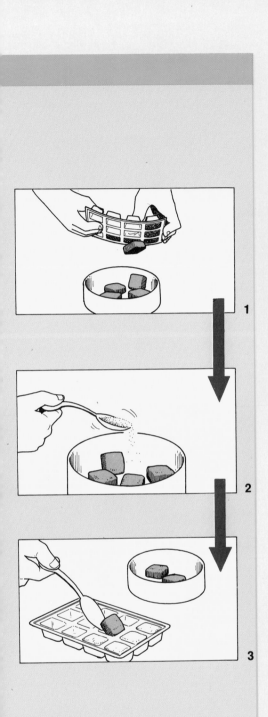

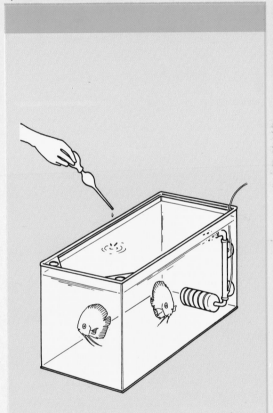

How to medicate by using discus "hamburger" food.
1) Thaw the "hamburger" and transfer it to a clean container.
2) Add 3 grams of PARAZAN (used with tropical fishes) to 100 grams of "hamburger" and mix thoroughly.
3) Freeze the portions again and feed them to the fish.

Medicinal bath. Put about 5 ml PARAZAN-D for aquatic use into about a 50-liter aquarium. A 60-cm tank contains about 50 liters of water. About 5 ml PARAZAN is a volume equal to 2 teaspoons. A unit of PARAZAN-D contains 500 ml, which may supply 100 doses for a 60-cm tank.

COUNTER-MEASURES

Since the bacteria infect not only the skin but the entire body, oral administration of an antibacterial solution (such as Parazan) is desirable. If the fish is too weak to feed, add the medication to the water.

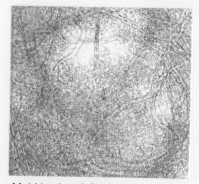

Mold hyphae infection on diseased body skin. Microphotograph (100X).

4. SAPROLEGNIA (FUNGUS DISEASE)

This disease is a fungus disease found in many freshwater fishes. It is also known as aquatic bacterial disease, cotton cover disease, or mouth fungus. The correct name is water fungus disease.

The characteristics of the disease are: growths of a cotton fiber-like shape appears to be attached to the skin or parts of the fins and parts of the fins or tail become dissolved or deteriorate. Conformably, the disease can be easily diagnosed externally, although its occurrence mechanism is complicated.

Usually contracted as a secondary disease atop an existing primary disease. The primary disease in this case would be an abrasion, external parasites, a bacteria or virus, and/or stress.

Furthermore, the disease is mostly contracted under lower water temperatures when the fish's physiological activity is low, but in the case of the discus it is necessary to be careful even under warmer water conditions.

SYMPTOMS

Cotton fiber-like growths are attached to parts of the skin. By scratching off part of the infected area and observing it, many thread-like strings (hyphae) can be seen. Such fine strings seen with the naked eye resemble cotton.

The hyphae that appear on the skin surface spread deep into the muscle tissue that will cause the fish to die due to the loss of osmotic pressure adjustment. Growth of the hyphae is rapid, killing the fish in 3-4 days after the cotton fiber-like hyphae are visible to the naked eye. At times, the cotton fiber-like hyphae will grow thickly on the skin but the fish will survive. In such a case, it is thought that it depends on the contracted fungi's origin or the body parts infected.

CAUSE

The disease is caused by true fungi, usually of the genera *Saprolegnia*, *Achyla*, and *Aphanomyces*. These genera belong to the water fungus family,

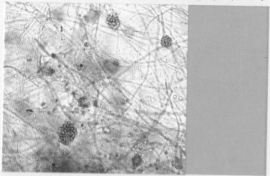

Massive numbers of zoospores seen among the hyphae (primary dormant spores). Microphotograph (100X).

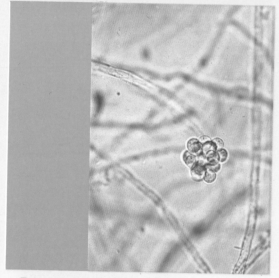

Enlargement of above photo. The massive dormant spores (zoospores) are formed on the end of zoosporangia, which means this is a fungus belonging to the genus *Aphanomyces*. Microphotograph (400X).

Saprolegniaceae, order Saprolegniales of the Oomycetes. The disease contracted in warm water temperatures is mostly caused by fungi of the genus *Aphanomyces*.

COUNTER-MEASURES

The infection originates from the zoospore released by the zoosporangium formed at the end of a hypha. Therefore, to stop the spread of the disease it is necessary to kill the zoospores. Also, to eliminate the prime cause it is necessary to eliminate the hyphae.

To eliminate the prime cause, immerse the infected fish in 0.5ppm of malachite green solution for about 30 minutes or in 2 to 3% saltwater for about 1 minute. For effective results, Green F, Sunace, or Methylene Blue liquid solutions are also effective.

5. FRESHWATER WHITE SPOT DISEASE

This disease can be contracted when there is some kind of stress inflicted on the fish such as decrease in water quality, overfeeding, overcrowded conditions, or moving the fish from one aquarium to another where the water temperature is not the same. Caution should be taken because once the disease is contracted it will rapidly spread and infect other fish in the aquarium.

Freshwater fishes kept in water temperatures under 20°C usually are more susceptible to the

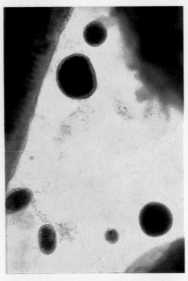

Large and small white-spot (ich) disease organisms appearing on a gill. Microphotograph (40X).

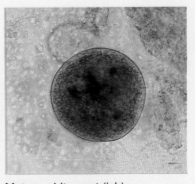

Mature white-spot (ich) organism, *Ichthyophtherius multifiliis*. Microphotograph (100 X).

disease. If the disease is contracted, raise the water temperature to 30°C as one preventive measure. The white spot parasite will not breed at this temperature.

From this, it is generally said that if the discus is kept in waters around 28-32°C, it is safe from the white spot disease. But actually, the disease can be contracted even at these temperatures. If this happens, it is important to gradually raise the water temperature to 34°C. The white spot parasite infecting tropical fishes has developed a tolerance to and can breed at higher temperatures.

SYMPTOMS

Diagnosis of the infected fish is easily made because many white spots can be seen on the skin and fins with the naked eye. The white spot parasite can also invade the gills, in which case it can kill many

fish before it is discovered. Generally, after the white spot parasite is noticed on the skin, it will gradually, and at times rapidly, weaken the fish and kill it.

CAUSE

Caused when many *Ichthyophtherius multifiliis*, hymenostome protozoans, invade the gills or skin of the fish. The young parasite will swim in the water waiting for a chance to invade the host. When this parasite finds the right time, it will infiltrate right above the basal membrane which is located under the gills epidermal tissue or of the skin and fins. There it will feed on such things as decaying epidermal cells, moving itself around by ciliary movement, and grow.

A fully grown body of the parasite is of a somewhat round shape, most measuring about 0.5 to 0.8 mm in diameter, with a

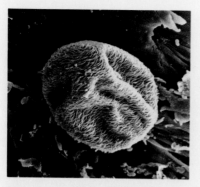

Mature *I. multifiliis*. Scanning electron microphotograph.

large horseshoe-shaped nucleus. After the fully grown protozoan leaves its host, it will transform into a cyst in the water and start to divide, producing many young parasites with cilia measuring from 0.03 to 0.05 mm in length. The propagation of the white spot disease is through the water by a multiplicative type of propagation during the young parasite's swimming period.

COUNTER-MEASURES

As mentioned before, increase of the water temperature is the effective treatment. If positively treating the disease, immersing the infected fish in 250 ppm formalin solution (dilute over the counter solution to 1:4000) for 30 minutes is the effective method. Methylene blue, Green F, Tropical Gold, and New Life solutions are also effective. However, the treatment only works against young parasites and will not work against grown parasites in the epidermal tissue. Therefore, it is necessary to repeatedly conduct the treatment to successfully eliminate the white spot disease.

6. INTESTINAL FLAGELLATES

From November, 1986, until the end of the following year an epidemic of unknown cause spread among the discus (it apparently has been occurring frequently since then). While searching for its cause, it was discovered that many *Hexamita*-like flagellates (a type of protozoan) had invaded the intestines of the affected fish. Such flagellates were thought to be the cause of the disease.

But further studies showed abnormalities in the kidneys and ureter of the affected fish, raising the possibility that this could be the direct cause of death. The cause of the abnormalities in the kidneys is still unknown. To ascertain whether or not the flagellate found in the intestines is either a *Hexamita* or a *Spironucleus* is very difficult, requiring an expert in the field to identify it. However, even if the infection was caused by a parasite of a different kind, symptoms and treatment are basically the same. So they are both considered here as intestinal flagellate disease.

Many flagellates are parasitic in the intestinal tract of fishes. Tissue photograph (H & E stained, 1000X).

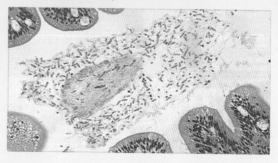

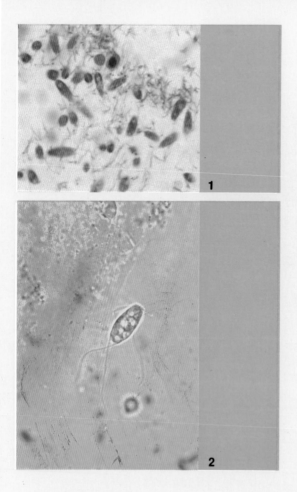

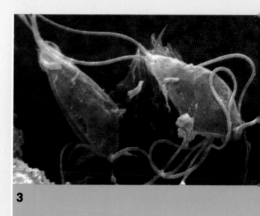

1. Enlargement of flagellate parasitic in the intestinal tract. Microphotograph (1000X).
2. Enlarged flagellate. Microphotograph (1000X).
3. Enlarged flagellate. Scanning electron microphotograph.

SYMPTOMS

It is commonly known that a discus becomes darker (blackish) during the course of breeding, as previously mentioned. In Germany, the *Hexamita*-disease has long been known as a prominent disease of discus; in Japan, the disease had not been too much of a problem. Lately, though, cases of intestinal flagellate disease have increased.

Symptoms are that the fish will turn darker in color, weaken, will not swim actively, and will not feed. In a chronic case the fish will become gaunt and lose its back muscles. It can also become anemic.

CAUSE

The intestinal flagellates found in the affected fish reproduce in large numbers, sometimes being of only one kind and sometimes of two. The flagellate parasite is believed to be *Hexamita intestinalis* or *Spironucleus elegans*.

Taxonomically, it is difficult to distinguish which one is the culprit, but with the information that the *Hexamita* nucleus is oval and the *Spironucleus* nucleus is of a sausage shape and that there is a crack at the nucleus' side only in *Hexamita*, the distinction can be made. In general, the confirmation of a parasite with six flagella in front and two in the rear making rapid movements in the intestines should be sufficient.

Spironucleus elegans is a parasite known to infect not only discus but also the intestines of angelfish, carp, and amphibian species. This parasite can move from the intestines to other parts of the body, where it is said to cause swelling of the gall bladder, but details are unknown. The infected fish is said to drag a whitish stringy feces from its anus. In such cases, diagnosis can be made by looking for the existence of flagellates in the feces.

COUNTER-MEASURES

Treatment is needed when more than 20 flagellates are found when observing part of the intestines or the feces under a microscope (100X). There are different methods for treatment, but mixing 20 to 30 mg of Metronidazole to each kilo of weight of the fish with its food and administering it for 2-3 days is sufficient.

7. *CHILODONELLA*

This is a parasitic disease found not only in discus but in many other species of freshwater tropical fishes, frequently occurring when a type of *Chilodonella* parasite invades the surface of the gills and

1. Many ciliated protozoan parasites seen between the gill filaments. Microphotograph (200X).
2. *Chilodonella* breeding on the gill surface. Microphotograph (400X).
3. Enlargement of a protozoan parasite (*Chilodonella*). Microphotograph (1000X).
4. Parasites on the surface of a gill. Scanning electron microphotograph.
5. Ventral side of parasite, showing lines of cilia. Scanning electron microphotograph.

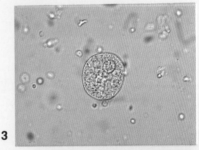

3

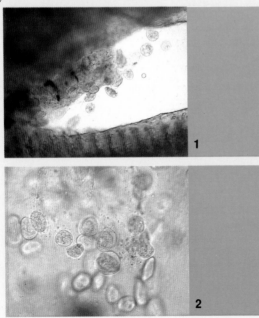

2

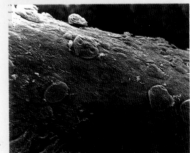

1

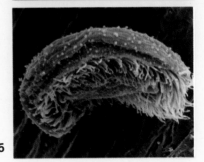

4

5

reproduces there. The parasite is too small to be seen with the naked eye. When many parasites invade, there will be an abnormal secretion of mucus and decay of the skin caused by the irritation, resulting in fatal respiratory disorder. Take immediate treatment measures if there is a possible *Chilodonella* infection.

SYMPTOMS

Because no abnormalities are noticeable from external appearance or swimming pattern, it is necessary to directly observe part of the gills under a microscope to know if the parasite is there. In general, when the gills are infected by a different agent, this parasite will feed on the infected area's decayed cells and other bacteria which multiplied there, using these for nourishment to reproduce. At this time the parasite will stimulate its host by sucking in its stomach area, sticking on the gill's surface. This parasite may also be found on healthy fish, but there is no concern if the number of parasites found is low.

CAUSE

Caused by *Chilodonella hexasticha*, which is a ciliated protozoan. This parasite is of an oval shape, measures from 30 to 40 microns in length, and has very active movements. When it is under a scanning microscope you will see that the stomach area is almost flat, with a small depression, and with 6 or 7 cilia lines on the left and right sides.

This specific parasite also lives on carp and goldfish, resembling *Chilodonella cyprini*, which at times can cause great harm. The difference is that *C. hexasticha* reproduces in warm temperatures (above 20°C) while *C. cyprini* reproduces in water temperatures ranging between 5° and 10°C. Also, *C. cyprini* invades the skin of its host and its body length is 30-40 microns, being a bit larger than *C. hexasticha*.

COUNTER-MEASURES

Immerse the infected fish in 250ppm formalin solution for 30 minutes. Proliferation of the parasite can be caused by bad water and poor environmental quality as well as by an infection of other large parasites (flukes) on the gills, necessitating great care in maintaining the aquarium.

8. MONOGENETIC FLUKES (GILL FLUKES)

The gill flukes are well known to breeders as one of the most frequent gill diseases contracted by the discus. Caused by the invasion of small flatworms known as flukes and belonging to the order Dactylogyridea. Further study shows that the parasite may belong to the genus *Ancyrocephalis*. At present, since the genus and species are not specifically known, it is simply called monogenean gill parasite disease.

SYMPTOMS

The affected fish will float close to the surface of the aquarium and will stay immobile, with no strength, showing abnormal behavior. Also, the opening and closing of the gill covers (breathing) will be faster than normal. The skin will be darker than its actual color. These

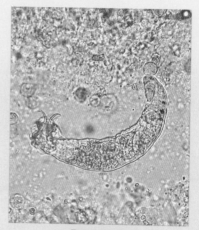

Parasitic fluke from gill. Microphotograph (200X).

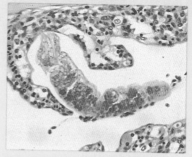

Parasitic fluke attached to gill filament. Tissue photograph (H & E stained, 200X).

Monogenean fluke on gill filament. (Parasite has a pair of "eyes".) Microphotograph (200X).

Marginal hooks of a monogenean parasite.

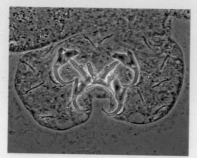

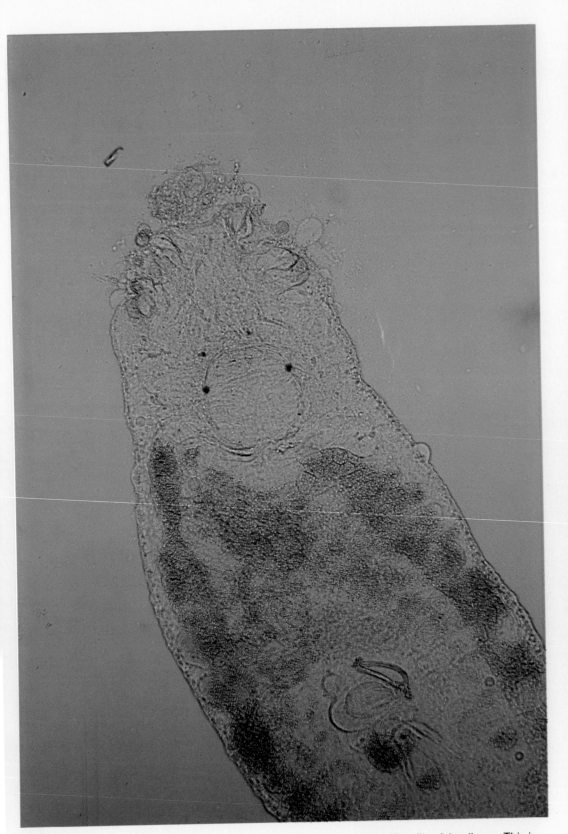

Dactylogyrus sp., a monogenetic fluke or trematode that lives mainly on the gills of the discus. This is the anterior end showing the suckers and "eye" spots.

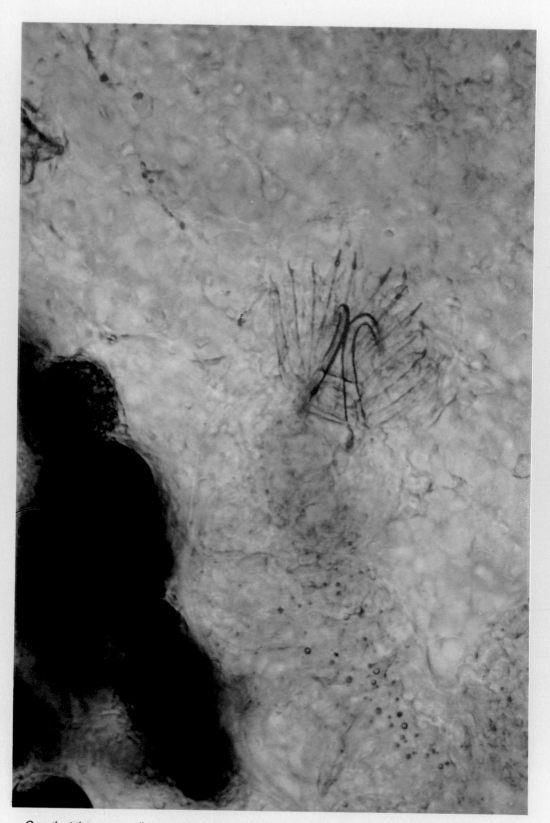

Gyrodactylus sp. usually parasitize the skin of the fish, more rarely the gills. This is the posterior end showing the two large central hooks surrounded by 16 smaller hooks used for attachment.

characteristics are caused by the invasion of the gills by many monogenean parasites. It is important to treat early or the fish will die shortly if left uncared for.

CAUSE

These gill parasites are classified under the monogeneans of the family Ancyrocephalidae. Parasite characteristics are that it has two anchors, two bars, and many marginal hooks at the front end. Species not identified.

COUNTER-MEASURES

Immerse affected fish in 250ppm formalin solution for 30 minutes. A better effect will be obtained by repeating this method after 4 or 5 days. Pay great attention to maintaining the aquarium since poor water and environmental quality are the causes for the parasite's explosive reproduction.

9. *CAPILLARIA*

This is a parasitic disease caused by the invasion of the discus' intestines by a large number of a specific kind of *Capillaria* species of roundworm (nematode). There is not much known about the infection period, frequency, effect, or adequate countermeasures.

By studying the intestines of a fish that shows darkening of the skin or inactivity, *Capillaria* was found in larger proportions when compared to healthy fish. It is a few millimeters long and is visible to the naked eye. Nematodes classified under this genus are known to live in the intestines of many different kinds of fishes, with seven different kinds reported found in tropical fishes.

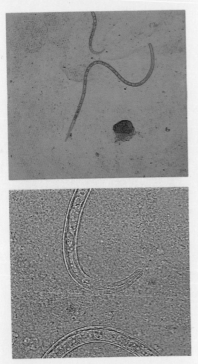

Intestinal roundworms.
Microphotograph (20X).

Enlargement of a part of a roundworm. Microphotograph (100X).

SYMPTOMS

The host fish will not show any external signs, making it difficult to know of the worm's existence in the discus' intestines. Because it is normal to check the discus' intestines when it dies in order to find out the cause of death, that is the only way and time we can be aware of the worm's existence there.

Even if worms are discovered, the direct cause of death is usually something else. Therefore, a more thorough study should be conducted. But, when a large number of worms are found in the intestines it is possible the fish became weak from indigestion and/or loss of appetite.

CAUSE

Capillaria sp. is a kind of roundworm classified under family Capillariidae. Parasites of this genus have string-like bodies and have no clear external characteristics.

The male parasite has a copulatory spicule or needle (thin and long, having weak chitin at times; its sheath is protruded and smooth, having a wall at times and is spineless) and its anus is located at the end or near the end of its body. The eggs are barrel-shaped with lids at each end. *Capillaria pterophylli* was reported found in angelfish, a close relative of the discus.

COUNTER-MEASURES

None known.

A group of intestinal worms. Tissue photograph (H & E stained, 100X).

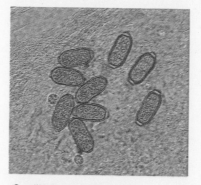

Capillaria eggs, showing characteristic barrel shape. Microphotograph (200X)

10. RODLET CELLS

After studying a discus whose color had darkened and whose appetite was poor, a large number of parasite-like objects were discovered inside its arteries. At first these objects were presumed to be some kind of protozoan, but because they were also found in the arteries of healthy, normal discus, it was decided that these were cells originally found in the fish.

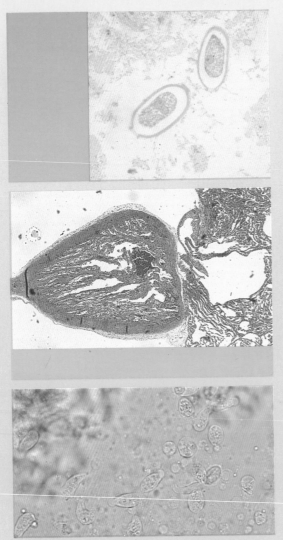

Roundworm eggs, enlarged, showing characteristic barrel shape. Tissue photograph (H & E stained, 400X).

Arterial ball. The ventricle of the heart is partially visible to the left. Tissue photograph (H & E stained, 40X).

Many rodlet cells are visible in the arterial ball. Microphotograph (400X).

CAUSE

These objects are called rodlet cells. Their function is not yet clearly understood. They seem to be found in larger quantities in fish showing some kind of abnormality rather than in healthy fish. Some researchers believe they are some kind of protozoan. The size of a rodlet cell found inside the artery measured from 6-7 by 12-13 microns. They were not found in the atrium nor in the ventricle but only in the artery.

11. GASTRECTASIA.

Gastrectasia can be found in different species of fishes at times and it is also called "abdominal inflation" because of its characteristics. But the name abdominal inflation is not correct due to different causes of the disease. In general, an abdominal inflation is caused by collected abdominal dropsy, swelling of the swim bladder or internal organs, or inflation of the intestines. Gastrectasia occurs when the stomach becomes abnormally inflated.

SYMPTOMS

It is easy to notice the abnormality because of the swelling in the abdominal area. The affected fish exhibits no appetite, will slowly weaken, its color will darken, and its swimming activity will decrease. Its abdominal area will feel too hard to have a collection of abdominal dropsy and too soft for a swelling in the internal organs, being easy to know there's an abnormal inflation of the stomach.

CAUSE

A kind of constipation caused by indigestion, meaning that for some reason food was not processed from the stomach to the intestines. Therefore, dilation of the stomach could have been caused by a large amount of food clogged there or by the clogged food having abnormally fermented there. Whichever the cause, the correct reason is unknown.

COUNTER-MEASURES

Not known. An effective method may be to stop feeding and prevent a secondary contraction.

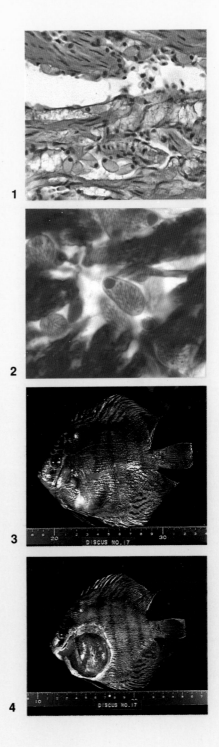

1. Many rodlet cells seen in arterial ball. Microphotograph (H & E stained, 400X).
2. Enlarged endothelia of arterial ball. Tissue photograph (Alizarin stained, 1000X).
3. External appearance of a diseased fish with a swollen belly.
4. Internal view of diseased fish with its stomach remarkably swollen.

According to some experts one of the secrets to successful discus raising and breeding is to overcome their initial shyness. Here some young Degen discus show that they are not shy at all.

THE BASICS OF DISCUS KEEPING

Selective breeding and hybridizing are the cornerstones of the tropical fish hobby. Many kinds of fishes (for example bettas, guppies, platies, and angelfishes) are the results of these procedures.

Discus recently have been the species that have been most newsworthy for their interbreeding and the creation of new varieties. No other species takes such a great amount of time or effort to interbreed.

Professional and amateur breeders in the U.S., Germany, Southeast Asia, Hong Kong, Japan, and other places around the world are doing research on discus propagation to fill the needs.

FIRST IMPORTS FROM THE UNITED STATES

It has been 20 years since we first saw discus on the tropical fish scene here in Japan. The first was a hybrid called the Powder Blue discus which was imported from the U.S. It had brilliant blue colors even on juveniles of 3 cm or less.

The "color discus" were imported from Southeast Asia. These discus are the forerunners of the Red Royal Blue (in my opinion they are the same fish). Importers and retailers maintained that the color discus were very popular and the aquarists reported that when they matured they become

the blue discus. From that time on, any discus that turned blue captured the interest of the aquarist.

The colors exhibited by discus can be shown off best under proper lighting conditions.

Many discus were dying, however, because people believed the discus needed freshwater high in acidity. Many discus died in spite of everything done to prevent it.

114

Two more entries to AQUARAMA '89 showing a range from a solid color to a fully striped strain.

WATTLEY TURQUOISE DISCUS CHANGED OUR OPINIONS ON DISCUS

People were excited about the color discus and Powder Blue discus until Jack Wattley developed the Wattley discus and succeeded in maintaining the strain.

In Japan some hobbyists read about this wonderful new strain of discus in *Tropical Fish Hobbyist* magazine. In 1980 only a few specimens of the Wattley Turquoise discus made their way into Japan through the efforts of a few local importers.

The adult discus, 12 to 16 cm in size, had a deep turquoise green color all over the body and elicited a stronger interest than previous varieties. It was a surprise to everyone that discus could change so much for the better.

Mr. Jack Wattley, who visited Japan for the first time in 1980, gave culture shock to the Japanese tropical fish industry. He had unique ideas about the nitrate cycle and water chemistry, aquariums, raising discus, and new food (discus "hamburger"), etc. All this was enough to change the old way of thinking for the Japanese.

Later, discus having turquoise green color were imported from Germany in large quantities. At first they were all classified as "Dutch Turquoise," as they had no specific names. Later, as more were imported, they used a mixture of English and German names to introduce the varieties.

Jack Wattley is constantly being asked to lecture on his methods of keeping and breeding discus. Here he is at a Holiday Inn unselfishly sharing his "secrets."

A beautiful Southeast Asian variety. Is the lack of red eyes due to some defect, or is it just the angle of the light.

These are some prize-winning discus that were bred in Southeast Asia. The high-fins are much more prized in Asian countries than they are in Europe or North America.

More prize-winning discus from AQUARAMA '89. Note the extensions of some of the soft rays in the dorsal and anal fins. These fish have maintained their brilliant colors in spite of being in bare tanks.

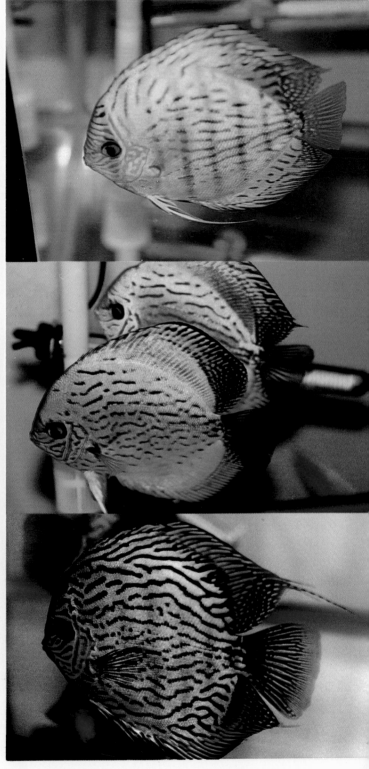

A beautiful deep-bodied discus from AQUARAMA '89. The red eye contrasts beautifully with the blue body color.

DECLINE OF DISCUS POPULARITY

For a while, we received all varieties of inbred strains. The amateur breeders were changing water every 1 or 2 days and feeding discus "hamburger" as the main diet. Amateur breeders had increased in numbers all over Japan. Discus popularity reached a peak, and whenever I went to aquarium shops I would see RRB and Dutch Turquoise in every shop. Also, I would see breeding equipment, home made "hamburger," artificial foods, and equipment for raising discus.

The importation of many strains of discus still continued. One strain imported from Singapore had regular lines on the body. It was called "Lichen Turquoise." Also, an attractive turquoise discus was imported from Malaysia, but it needed more work on its color. Due to further breeding and interbreeding, this strain has now disappeared.

The blue stripes have all but obliterated the background color of this strain. Some discus breeders prefer to accent the reddish color of the body and reduce the blue.

These are more prize-winning discus that were bred in Singapore and Malaysia. These are some of the solid colors. The upper fish are of a very unusual strain.

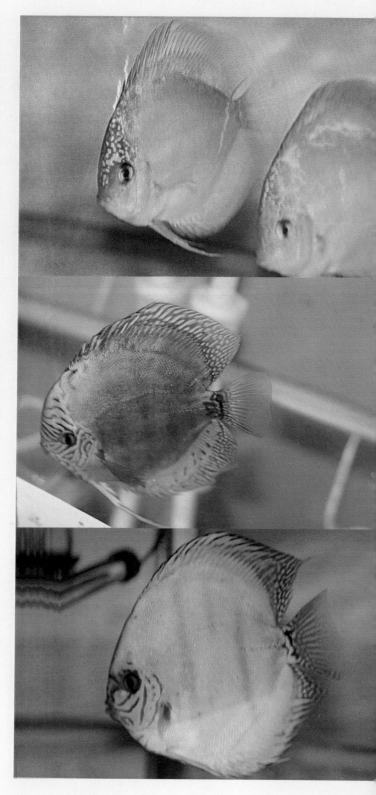

More solid color Singapore and Malaysian prize-winners. The pattern on the face makes a very nice contrast and gives the fish added personality.

At that time people could see discus in many *Tropical Fish Hobbyist* magazines. Because of the discus, the tropical fish hobby was very popular—but its popularity would soon decrease.

In late 1986 a discus disease that had no apparent cure swept Japan. The fish became dark and stayed on the bottom of the tank and would die in a few days. Such an awful disease!

Aquarists who were keeping discus had a variety of theories, but this panic continued for over half a year. Because of this disease, the popularity of discus decreased. It was later learned that the disease came from the discus raised and exported from Southeast Asia.

Some experts say that the shape of the head is very important in breeding. With the wrong shape the discus is said to be unable to see its eggs and therefore cannot tend them.

Many of the shops in Japan experimented with cures and had good success. The disease is no longer a problem.

In 1988, Mr. Bernd Degen, who is a discus specialist, visited Japan for a second time and gave seminars throughout our country. His expertise on the subject excited the Japanese aquarists. He introduced discus strains from many countries to the aquarists in Germany. He told the Japanese discus hobbyists that there was no need to worry.

THE DISCUS SCENE CHANGES AGAIN

Mr. Degen published many articles in aquarium magazines. One title was "Discus Crazy," which was published 30 times. From writing this article, he discovered that there were many serious discus hobbyists in Japan. At the same time, I found that there are discus breeders and discus professionals in Japan who are trying to surpass the achievements of the U.S. and Germany.

Mr. Hitsu Shuichi of the Discus Institute, Mr. Abe Mitsuyoshi of Matsukawaya (who developed a unique strain), Mr. Awaya Kimihiro of Awaja, Mr. Nakamura Kazu, Mr. Yamana Munehish of Aqua Japan, Mr. Hirosi Akizo, and others are building their reputations as discus breeders.

Turquoise discus bred in Japan

were introduced from breeders all over Japan. The high quality solid turquoise from Japanese breeders are as good as the best German turquoise. These are strong bodied fish thanks to Japanese breeding. Demand for Japanese turquoise discus will no doubt continue to increase. I feel as though the Japanese discus scene has changed twice since Mr. Wattley's trip to Japan.

Most of the imported discus are offered as show fish in Japan. The original discus are imported with great care. I wonder if it is time to think about the ways and means of raising discus now. For example, we need enough space for the discus to swim. I wish you are able to observe the solid turquoise at length and at the same time think about the equipment so you can improve your knowledge of the discus, the king of tropical fishes.

All successful discus breeders take personal interest in their discus. Bernd Degen scrutinizes a batch of babies as they are being fed brine shrimp nauplii.

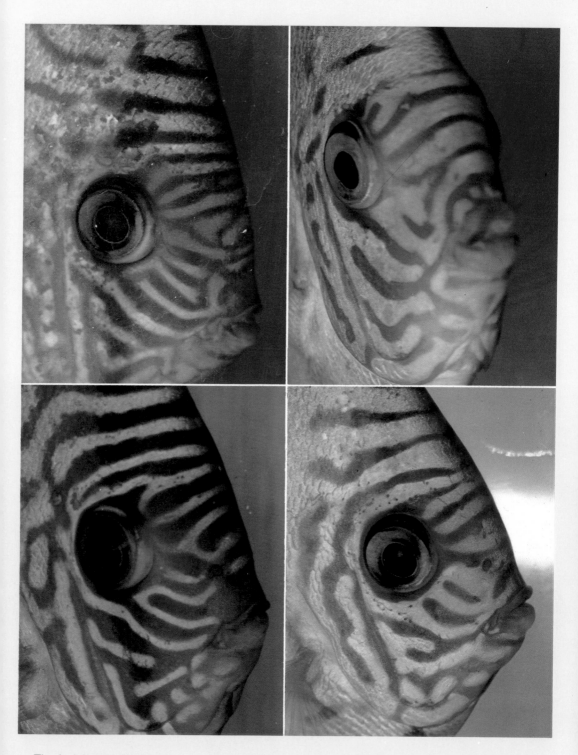

The facial patterns of discus are so unique one can identify individual discus by just noting certain characteristics of the pattern. The color of the eye is also important to some breeders, with a bright red eye highly favored

A Degen turquoise discus with a high fin.

In Thailand you may commonly see discus with very elongate middle dorsal fin rays. Like the high-fin discus, some like this type, others do not.

In this Singapore strain the red has become enhanced so much that the blue has virtually become lost (aside from the pattern itself).

ORIGINAL SPECIES AND CULTIVATED STRAINS

THE CLASSIFICATION OF THE ORIGINAL SPECIES OF DISCUS

The original wild-type discus were collected in the Amazon basin and, as of today, there are several subspecies. People are interested in the original discus because of its natural coloration, which is different from the interbred strains that are solid blue.

I cannot say much definitely about discus classifications because they concern the distant wild Amazon River. As invoices from German exporters show, the original discus can now be classified into 14 varieties. Let me introduce these discus to you.

HECKEL BLUE DISCUS - *SYMPHYSODON DISCUS* (1 species, 2 subspecies, 5 strains).

Distribution: Rio Negro, Rio Trombetas, Rio Madeira, and Albuquerque River.

Its body is brown and gray-brown and it has narrow horizontal blue stripes covering the whole body. The blue shines slightly but under good aquarium conditions it becomes a beautiful sky blue. We can say it is not brightly colored but it is a discus that has a pleasant disposition.

The fifth dark vertical bar that we see in the middle of the body is the most noticeable characteristic of this species. Later, we will refer to this as the Heckel band. It also has arc-shaped dark lines (the black arch) on the fins and tail. This black arch is not very distinct and under good conditions these lines will almost disappear. The eyes are dark brown or vaguely orange. It is rare to see strong red color in the eyes even when the fish is in its spawning colors.

Heckel discus are said to be the most delicate and timid. Recently, however, the conditions for their importation have improved and we can expect them to live a long life once they eventually settle down to aquarium life. But it is certain that in a mixed aquarium the Heckel discus will not accept food due to fear of the other fishes or loud noises and will turn dark and hide in the corner of the aquarium. It is best to raise them in a discus-only aquarium containing 3 to 5 individuals.

In 1981 five varieties were recognized from the differences in the lines on the body. There are two recognized subspecies: *S. discus discus*, which has 45 to 53 scale rows, and *S. discus willischwartzi*, has 53 to 59 scale rows.

Symphysodon discus discus is distributed in the Rio Negro, which flows from the north to the Amazon River; *S. discus willischwartzi* is from the Rio Madeira, which flows from the south to the Amazon River. It is difficult to distinguish between these two subspecies by appearance alone. Heckel Blue discus are imported from South America through the U.S. or directly into Japan. In Germany, it is classified into six varieties besides the Heckel Blue. These six varieties include the High Form Blue Head, which has a different shape and color.

You want to keep it in mind that you should maintain the water temperature at 27° to 30°C and keep the nitrogen compounds low. The breeding of this species is the most difficult of all the discus. The adult is 15 to 18 cm. Crossbreeding with turquoise discus was popular before, but in 1988 Mr. Awajiya Kimihiro of Awajiya in Osaka, bred and raised Heckel discus. The thick dark bars that are characteristic of the species can show up in RRB (which do not have the bloodline of the Heckel Blue) and the original discus.

GREEN DISCUS - *SYMPHYSODON AEQUIFASCIATA AEQUIFASCIATA*

Distribution: Lago Tefé and Rio Tefé, Santarem, and the Peruvian Amazon.

This is a beautiful discus which has a yellowish brown body with green horizontal stripes from head to tail. The green shows up very brightly around the base of the tail in contrast to the black arch. The eyes have a strong red color, which is one of the most attractive points of the subspecies. It is also a trait in the interbred turquoise. It is desirable to have these characteristics combined with a metallic blue body. This subspecies can be subdivided by location: the Peruvian green, which has red spots on its body, and the Tefe green, which does not but has stripes from the head to the fins and around the tail, are well known. It is not easy to separate the subspecies of *Symphysodon aequifasciata*. Each person will have his own opinion of their validity and the means of distinguishing them. The discus that have more green coloration and stripes are called Royal Green Discus. This variety is very expensive because of its popularity. Green discus are very easy to import and can be readily purchased. They are not difficult to find at a size of 15 cm or larger. In an aquarium you can have a reasonable chance for success in spawning them as the discus of today are imported in better condition.

BLUE DISCUS – SYMPHYSODON AEQUIFASCIATA HARALDI
Distribution: Leticia (Peru), Benjamin Constant, and Purus Rivers, Manacapuru, etc.

The original type has a basic color that is reddish brown and has blue stripes from the head to the bases of the fins and around the tail. The blue stripes may vary due to the location and between individual specimens. Sometimes there is blue on the forehead and wavy lines and spots. The Royal Blue has stripes all over. It is quite variable. Among the original species it has an "unfixed" form. It is not too much to say that the existence of this subspecies is confusing the classification of the species.

The amount of blue color that shows up at the base of the tail helps separate these and the green variety. On a green discus stripes are double and the basic color has spots; on the blue discus the stripes are clear. They were imported with green discus before, but recently high quality blue discus or Royal Blue Discus have been imported in large quantities. If you keep the water between 27° and 30° C and nitrate levels low, then it is easy to raise them. You have a better chance to breed them when you keep 5 or 6 specimens in a 90 cm aquarium. This is the easiest subspecies to breed next to the brown discus.

BROWN DISCUS – SYMPHYSODON AEQUIFASCIATA AXELRODI
Distribution: Around Belem and Urubu Rivers, around Manaus.

This is the most popular of the original discus. The brown discus of 2 to 3 cm found in Japan are mostly raised in Hong Kong, Thailand, and Singapore. These fish are bred from discus also bred and raised in areas other than the Amazon.

Germany is a large exporter of brown discus, which are sometimes sold as Simon Discus. Because of the cost of exporting and fish value, Japan does not import directly from Germany.

Breeders of brown discus in Hong Kong are now gathering in the New Territories, where tropical fishes are now starting to be raised. They are using slight aeration in hundreds of aquaria of 45 x 45 x 45 cm that are without filters or equipment for breeding. Each mated pair of discus lays eggs on the glass of the aquarium. Around 100 mated pairs are always laying eggs, and each female will lay from 200 to 300 eggs at a time. This way breeders can mass produce.

Only a few wild brown discus are exported in shipments of other tropical fishes from the Amazon into Japan. They have a strong red base color. Blue always shows up on the head, fins, and tail, but the red base color is the most attractive.

This is the subspecies that breeds most easily among the original species and subspecies. Especially the ones bred in Hong Kong and Southeast Asia can adjust well to the water. That is why, if we can get a mated pair, it will be easy to breed and raise brown discus. These are, therefore, the best discus to practice breeding on or to interbreed. Also, you can get valuable experience in raising the fry. I think it is best for the beginner to start with 1 to 10 specimens at a time and find out through experience how to raise them. Fry of the brown discus are very inexpensive.

THE PRESENT STATUS OF DISCUS VARIETIES

Jack Wattley Turquoise

This is the variety that Mr. Jack Wattley of the U.S. has developed. It is also the most famous among the turquoise discus. The breeders are selected from the beautifully colored specimens of *Symphysodon aequifasciata axelrodi* that are gathered from around the middle of Jura River in the Amazon. The origin of the present Turquoise Discus that are kept and bred is from the selection and separation of the best turquoise colors in the fins and interbreeding the specimens to maintain the colors.

By the seventh generation this type of color will be maintained. Until now, 17 generations have been raised. The most popular ones in Japan are those we call the "Third Generation." They have very thick turquoise green stripes with the basic colors showing up between the stripes.

Compared to the Dutch Turquoise, this shiny turquoise green is superior because of its deep intense color. Sometimes juveniles the size of half dollars are imported. But these specimens tend to be delicate, so it is necessary that we be careful with the quality of the water and the raising procedures.

The Wattley Highfin Full Body Discus are becoming the top of the Jack Wattley Turquoise line by taking the place of the Third Generation strain. It seems they have the blood of German or Hong Kong Turquoise (Hong Kong Turquoise of Mr. Lo Yin Yat). They give quite a different impression from the Third Generation Turquoise. They have red eyes and the fins and tail are rather large. Most specimens have blue all over the body ("Full Body"). By interbreeding we can improve the strain to show more of the Third Generation Turquoise. This will produce the perfect turquoise.

Another type is called the "First Generation" Turquoise. This one is similar to the Dutch Pearl Turquoise. On the side of the body there are blue spots and the body becomes large. But it is not imported frequently and we do not see it very often. At one time there was an interruption in the egglaying because of a collapse in quality of the head, gills, and even the entire body, but recently it has improved.

DUTCH TURQUOISE

These are very popular among the Turquoise Discus breeders. Up until this time there are over 200 German discus breeders. Many types of discus are bred. According to the price lists, there are 14 varieties being sold today. There are no identifying descriptions of the varieties on price lists or instructions on how to maintain them. Therefore, when

you buy them, you do not have to be concerned about the names on the price lists.

You can choose the ones you like by observing the quality of the color on the gill covers and the intensity of blue on the head and around the fins. Also, the quality of blue around the fins and tail is important.

For your reference, I will now describe the characteristics of the strains most frequently imported (including the names for Japan only) below.

• **Cobalt Blue Turquoise**: As you can see from the name, it is the deepest color available among the Dutch Turquoise. The ones imported into Japan are juveniles between 3 to 4 cm and up to 8 cm. All are intensely colored. These have a higher percentage with turquoise blue all over the body when they are 8 cm in size, but when they are 3 to 4 cm there are many variations. Royal Cobalt Flash or Cobalt Flash is the one that exhibits more beautiful blue and the most expensive one among the Dutch Turquoise. Metallic Cobalt (an electric blue which has metallic colors) are sometimes imported and they are high quality fish.

• **Radiant Turquoise**: This is the one that is similar to the Cobalt Blue Turquoise. Its color is reddish, which is typical of German Turquoise. Some of those with stripes are more beautiful than the full color varieties. Most individuals imported are 4 to 5 cm in size. When we buy the fish it is better to choose according to color rather than by name. If you want to breed them, it is best to start with 10 strong healthy specimens.

• **Full Color Turquoise**: Before it was developed as a strain, some individuals were imported at 3-4 cm. Its handling of color is not as good as in other varieties. One of its selling points is its price, being the cheapest of the Dutch Turquoise. It could be recommended as a variety for beginners. We can enjoy our money's worth when we choose carefully by the shape and the size of the fins and brilliance of body color. There are some so beautiful that they give us enjoyment in spite of the price.

• **Pearl Red Turquoise; Pearl Blue Turquoise**: The meaning of the name given to this variety of turquoise is that the stripes appear as tightly spaced pearls. The ones bred by Schmidt-Focke are the most famous and have a tremendous popularity. Most of the juveniles of 3-4 cm from striped turquoise do not have much of the characteristics of the original Schmidt-Focke discus.

There are so many monotone blue discus because of the strength of the color. They don't give us any idea of the color of the adult at this size. Therefore, the color of the juveniles and adults are very different, but you can recognize the good ones by the shape.

• **Red Turquoise**: This is a striped turquoise that has reddish brown as its basic color (which happens to be characteristic of the original discus). It is different from the secondary red color of the body. The reddish brown color of this strain is close to a brick red color and I think it will become more popular later.

The ones that are imported are mostly 3-4 cm juveniles. They are hard to distinguish from the brilliant type. We can expect the importation of specimens of 8 cm or more.

* **Bernd Degen Turquoise**: This is a Dutch Turquoise which is bred by Mr. Bernd Degen, who is a discus specialist from Germany. Four or five varieties are imported, such as Red Turquoise, Royal Cobalt Flash, Cobalt Turquoise, etc. There are some German breeders who are breeding turquoise that are imported into Japan and the breeders are not very good. Therefore, there are some discus varieties that are available, the reasons for their existence not being very clear. But Mr. Degen's turquoise gives us no problems on this point. I think it will be more necessary to develop a system that shows a better way to import the fish. Like those from Dr. Schmidt-Focke, Dr. Zigfried Homan, Horst Bitter, etc., I hope direct imports from the top breeders in Germany will increase.

HONG KONG TURQUOISE

Since the spring of 1986, we have been receiving inexpensive turquoise discus in large quantities from Singapore, Malaysia, and Thailand, following Jack Wattley and German Turquoise. On the tropical fish scene, where people try to import more and more fishes while they are popular, many species are being imported in greater numbers and discus are not an exception. It is sad that Southeast Asian shippers are thinking more in terms of quantity rather than quality, whereas Europe and the United States still think quality comes first. The Turquoise Discus bred in Thailand (Bangkok) and Malaysia (Penang) have disappointed the people from their poor handling of color and poor shape.

Eventually, it was Hong Kong that raised excellent turquoise, like the European and American varieties, by careful breeding and programmed selection. And Hong Kong is the closest breeding country to Japan. Groups of turquoise being raised by Mr. Lo Yin Yat (who is one of the writers of this book) and Mr. Simon Yim have excellent shape, body color, and price. Although there are some unclear points regarding the price list names sent to Japan, I would like to introduce some of the popular varieties.

• **Highfin Wattley Turquoise**: This Turquoise Discus is mostly raised in Hong Kong with a variety of sizes. They are very popular. 5-6 1/2 cm juveniles are readily imported. On many specimens they have grayish blue color on their bodies. I recommend this to the people who want to try to raise Turquoise Discus for the first time or to the people who are planning to raise discus in one or two years. Unless you get lazy in their daily care, they will grow to beautiful specimens.

• **Highfin Cobalt Blue Turquoise**: This is Dr. Lo Yin Yat's original type turquoise. Five to 15 cm individuals are all imported. In a U.S. magazine they are called Lo's Blue Turquoise. The original parents were called Dutch Brilliant Turquoise.

Presently, Schmidt-Focke Turquoise and Jack Wattley Turquoise blood have been mixed with Highfin Cobalt Blue Turquoise and the progeny are becoming similar to the Dutch Turquoise.

• **High Body Giant Turquoise, Highfin Giant Wattley Turquoise**: Only adults more than 15 cm are imported. They are called Giant Turquoise. It is not like the high body highfin of the price lists. The good thing about raising these fish is that they are cheap, so they are good for the breeders who do not want to start with juvenile specimens.

But at the same time there are risks. These are good for show but not for breeding purposes. You can get the adults with a high breeding percentage very easy so you have to accept this fact.

• **Remaining varieties**: I would like to present some of the price list names of the remaining varieties. People are afraid that these varieties cause some people to lose interest in discus because although they have different names there are difficulties in finding the particular varieties.

Blushing Cobalt Turquoise
Giant Red Turquoise
Schmidt-Focke High Body Turquoise
Highfin Brilliant Turquoise
Red Turquoise
Laser Green
65% Full Color Blue Metallic, etc.

Anyway, Hong Kong Turquoise have a high percentage that will get disease because of differences in the water quality immediately after being imported and up to one week after. It is important to have proper preventive measures when handling newly imported discus.

When you move them from plastic bags to aquariums, replace approximately one-third to one-half of the water in the bag with aquarium water. Leave them for 15 to 30 minutes, then drain one-third to one-half of the water from the bag and replace it with aquarium water. Repeat this three or four times. Anyway, try to allow them to adjust to the water quality of the aquarium—but do it slowly. We need at least two hours for this work.

You should avoid keeping newly imported discus with old specimens in your aquarium for two to three months because Japanese Turquoise and German Turquoise get diseased very easily compared to Hong Kong Turquoise.

RED ROYAL BLUE DISCUS

The RRB is bred and raised in Southeast Asia, especially in Bangkok, Thailand. A large number are imported, and it is one of the most popular discus in Japan. It exhibits bright red color all over the body and is very showy with various designs of blue stripes.

It has both wide and narrow blue stripes and spots and has good color all over the body. Each specimen is different. It is hard to tell the juveniles and adults apart by color. Therefore, if you want to raise the beautiful ones you better choose a specimen of 7 cm or larger.

The red color that this strain shows comes from lobster eggs and is caused by the carotene in the eggs. That is why if you don't feed the fish with a diet high in carotene, in several months it will lose its color. The foods that have the carotene include most freshwater shrimp, crayfish, krill, and frozen shrimp.

The blue color that they have clearly from the time that they are juveniles is due to the use of male hormones, and they will also lose their color in a few weeks. But the blue color becomes clear as the fish grows. If you keep the quality of the water good, you can maintain the color. Also, the Marine Blue Turquoise that has been crossed with the Dutch Turquoise is a new variety we can expect soon.

• **Red Discus**: This strain is imported from Bangkok, Thailand, and is very popular. But it is not an interbred strain. These are Blue Discus that initially exhibit a brilliant red color all over the body when fed the crustacean eggs. By its beautiful shape and the speed of its growth, this is the best discus for beginners compared to the same size brown discus. Also, the price is cheaper than most other strains except for the brown discus. Just like the RRB, if you keep giving food heavy in carotene you can enjoy the beautiful red color all over its body. Among the Southeast Asian interbred strains there are the Blue Face, Powder Blue, and 7-color Chemical Hong Kong Blue as well, but all of them disappear in time.

THE REMAINING DISCUS STRAINS

You can see that the interbred strains of discus are endless. That is why we cannot lose our concentration on the new strains from time to time. Among the tropical fish species, discus are at the top. Our interest in new strains never dies. Even at this moment there will be a new successful interbred strain somewhere. Finally, I want to tell you about the interbred strains presently available in Japan.

• **Matsukawaya Turquoise**: This is a type bred by Mr. Abe Mitsuyoshi of Matsukawaya in Tokyo. It was produced from interbreeding Dutch and Jack Wattley Turquoise. The amount and quality of maintenance necessary are high.

• **Shirase Thunder Flash**: This is a beautiful strain that was developed by interbreeding Dutch Turquoise and RRB by Mr. Shirase Akizo of Yokohama.

• **Fude Turquoise**: This is a strain that was raised by Mr. Fude Shuichi of Kanazawa, one of the authors of this book. It was developed from the Dutch Turquoise. There are no details or information on the names of strains. You just pick the one you like.

• **Heckel Cross Turquoise**: This strain was produced by Mr. Awajiya Kimihiro of Awajiya in Osaka by crossing a female Dutch Turquoise and a male Heckel Blue. It is expected to become a new variety.

• **Radical Blue Turquoise**: This is the one Mr. Yamana Munehish and Mr. Amano Munehiko are raising. It was developed from interbreeding Marine Blue from Bangkok and is a beautiful discus.

• **Half Heckel Discus (Wattley Crossbreed)**: This is a hybrid between the Royal Blue Discus bred by Mr. Jack Wattley and a Heckel Blue Discus.

136

- **Singapore Turquoise (Lichen Turquoise)**: This is an interbred strain of Singapore-bred discus. They were imported in numbers several years ago but the handling of the colors on the adult fish was not good. The blue color does not show up well. Presently, it is not imported into Japan.

- **Shirase Quarter Heckel Turquoise**: This is a discus strain that has been developed by crossbreeding Wattley Highfin Full Body and Wattley Crossbreed by Mr. Shirase in Yokohama.

- **Red Flash**: This is a hybrid. It is called Marine Blue (Neon Blue in the Kansai area) and not many are imported.

- **Lightning Turquoise**: This is an interbred strain produced from crossing Singapore Turquoise and Dutch Turquoise and was developed by Mr. Sawai Masayoshi of Marueikanstrigyo in Osaka. There are two types, red and blue. F_1 are sold presently.

BASIC DISCUS RAISING METHODS

基本的な飼育法

RAISING CONCEPT AND DAILY CARE (MR. FUMITOSHI MORI)

The discus is the hardest fish to raise and it is the king of tropical fishes. They have become so popular that we can see them in most of the aquarium stores. The number of strains has also increased.

The discovery and development of basic breeding and raising methods have made the discus very popular.

There are four important categories of knowledge for basic breeding of discus:
1. Quality of water.
2. Changing of water.
3. Feeding.
4. Capacity of selection and observation.

You cannot obtain this knowledge in a day, but it is not so much work that it would take years. Most important are daily observations and being patient.

OUTLINING THE RAISING CONCEPT

What is the purpose of raising discus? What is the proper way to raise them?
1. How much space do you have for aquaria?
2. How many aquaria do you have?
3. What do you use for a filter and heater?
4. How much can you afford to spend?
5. What strains are best for breeding and how many of them do you want to buy?
6. Is your purpose for raising fish to watch them or to breed them?

The space available and finances are most important.

Regarding the equipment for raising discus, you must concern yourself with filters, heaters, lights, and hoses (tubing) for changing water. Through experience gained by observing the equipment available for breeding discus, it is evident that you must use top quality equipment. Discus are very strong fish if you change the water enough. But if you keep too many fish in a small aquarium or if you use too small a filter, they do not do as well. No matter how much you spend for discus, half of your work is wasted.

I want you to know that the raising of discus for interbreeding and for display are basically different. When you raise discus for interbreeding, there are many rules to follow and you have to be careful all the time. But when you raise discus for show, it is possible to raise them in a lower quality of water. You don't need to raise them in a bare aquarium; you can raise them in an aquarium set up for display.

AQUARIUMS AND DISCUS QUALITY

Larger aquariums are better because then the water quality will stay good longer and the fish will have more oxygen and will not be as stressed as they would be in a small aquarium.

But there are few people who can have an aquarium larger than 180 cm base length to raise discus. That's why we have to use many different aquarium sizes depending on the quantities of fish to be kept. The size of the aquarium should match the size of the discus being kept. This will, of course, influence the aquarium maintenance.

Aquariums of 60 cm length suit the 3 to 5 cm juvenile fish. Standard aquariums of 60 x 30 x 30 cm sold in pet shops are good, but the best is slightly longer, 60 x 45 x 36 cm. We must use acrylic aquaria—about 100-liter capacity is best (the least being 60 liters).

The changing of the water and managing the water quality when it's new influences the intensity of colors on the fish and the shape of its body. The future of the 3 to 5 cm discus is decided by their daily care until they attain 8 cm in size. You need from 60 to 100 liters of water to keep water quality good if you do not want to spend lots of time on your aquarium. It's easy to keep 5 to 20 fish in this size aquarium. For juveniles over 8 cm in length, a depth of 36 cm decides their characteristics when they get larger, so you need at least 45 cm depth. Now it's time to move to a 75 to 90 cm aquarium.

In a 75 to 90 cm aquarium, the water capacity is 150 to 190 liters. We must use a higher grade of filter and heater, but it's much easier to maintain the water quality in this size aquarium than it is in a 60 cm aquarium.

It is easy to raise 5 to 10 fish in a 75 to 90 cm aquarium and, if your daily care is good, it is possible to keep from 20 to 30 fish in it. These 75 to 90 cm aquariums can be used as our main tanks for raising discus. If we have two or three of this size aquarium we can raise the fish from juveniles to adults and even get pairs. It is also possible to use these aquariums for interbreeding. You can obtain more varieties if you can get used to using these aquariums.

You need 90 to 120 cm tanks if you want to raise more than 10 fish of 12 cm size. Discus professionals keep these 120 cm aquariums all the time, but this aquarium size is a problem (although I don't say it's bad). But you need some additional knowledge in order to get used to it and maintain it successfully.

When you upgrade from 60 to 90 cm tanks there may be some hesitation, but you can handle this with better equipment. A top power filter and 200 watt heater will help the fish survive the winter in the smaller tank, but in a 120 cm aquarium this will not do. First of all, we need a special pump that has a higher water capacity instead of a smaller filter. We also need a large box filter. We need two 200 watt heaters. Besides all these, we need a sponge filter and a special air pump for secondary help. Even the glass cover required can be expensive. We can't be relaxed with our daily care. We need from 30 to 60 minutes to change water and there is a dominant and submissive relationship between the fish all of the time. Unless we solve these problems one by one, the dream 120 cm aquarium can be nothing.

If you understand the working of the large tank and know how to manage filter capacity and can adjust quantities of fish and dominant and recessive relationships, the situation of your discus will be much better. You can expect to receive more than you spend. So I want to advise the people who are planning to raise more than 10 adults to think about it. The average number of fish for a 120 cm aquarium is about 15 fish.

WATER QUALITY FOR RAISING DISCUS

People say slightly acid to neutral water is best to raise discus. Nitrites should be zero. Nitrites come from ammonia produced from fish waste and uneaten or rotten food. This ammonia can be changed to nitrites when the biological filter is working properly by *Nitrosomonus* bacteria, while *Nitrobacter* bacteria can change nitrites to nitrates, which are non-toxic. This means that if the filter is too small or the aquarium has too many fish in it, there will be ammonia and nitrites in the water.

Nitrites prevent the carrying of oxygen to the gills, so the fish will have breathing problems and excretion problems. The basics of raising discus includes thinking about the nitrites before you think about pH or water hardness. By having better filter equipment or by changing water you get rid of excess nitrites. There are very simple test kits available—you should use them.

Regarding pH, as long as it is not extremely acid (below 4) or extremely alkaline (over 8), you shouldn't have any problems. Only when you start breeding or one week after you add new fish to your aquarium do you need to be careful about pH. When the pH value is raised or lowered too fast, pH shock can occur, which removes too much body secretion from the skin and the internal organs and gills will be damaged.

As long as you use Japanese drinking water you don't have to worry about the pH. Currently hobbyists are also measuring GH and KH. They are using simple test kits that are available.

KH indicates the concentration of calcium and magnesium carbonates.

GH includes the concentration of compounds with other acids. Units are all indicated with this sign (°d). This sign (1°d) means it has 10 milligrams of minerals in 1 liter of water. In Japan most of the water is GH 4 to 7°d (soft water). KH is different at different locations, but the average is from 1 to 6. Therefore, you don't have to worry about the hardness except when you try to breed your discus.

CHANGING AND MAINTAINING WATER QUALITY

These days we are more concerned about the nitrites that come from fish waste and leftover food. To keep the discus in good conditions and disease-free, it certainly is necessary to improve the filtration and to think about diet, but regular partial water changes will help more directly.

Basic ideas to consider when changing water will be talked about separately.

During the time discus are juveniles (3 to 5 cm) it is most important to change water. The temperature should be from 30° to 32°C. The fish will want to eat all of the time, so you should feed the fish 3 to 5 times each day.

Therefore, the water will become dirty faster and the pH lower compared to similar setups at 30° or lower. In this situation, to maintain the discus in proper condition, changing water every day is necessary.

According to the number of fish or the capacity of the filter, the quantity of water changed will be

different. If the aquarium is 60 cm you should change two-thirds of the water. The way to change the water is by using a hose to siphon off excretion and uneaten food. After adding fresh neutralized water, stabilize the temperature.

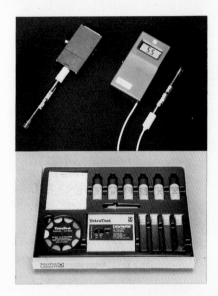

It is necessary to monitor your water quality. These pH test kits show two extremes—simple colorimetric kit and electrode measuring devices with digital readouts.

Some people say you should change half of the water once a week. But this is not acceptable for discus. Compared to the people who change water every day, there will be lots of difference in the fish. The concentration of nitrites in the juvenile's food affects the intensity of blue in the adult fish. It can be seen in the difference in the shape of the body so that we can determine whether or not the discus has been raised under unrestricted conditions.

Changing water is more important than quantity or quality of food in order to raise fish with good personalities. Juvenile fish at this time should have the eyes appear small compared to the body size.

The time before adulthood occurs at a size of from 6 to 9 cm. During this time I want you to start with less fish so that they will have room to swim. For a 90 cm tank, you should have approximately 10 fish. This is the time the blue color becomes stronger. You should increase the feeding of the discus "hamburger" as well as fish roe and artificial food during this period.

It is true that changing water less often during this time makes the blue color stronger, but you should remember that the adult discus reaches its peak at 12 cm. You shouldn't expect its full color before that size. We should make it our priority to build up the body during this time.

It is important for the filter system to work well no matter if the fish is a juvenile or an adult. This is especially true during the time before adulthood when the body circulation is good. For example, don't just think about using the top filter alone. Use a power filter, a sponge filter, etc., all at the same time, and try other filters also.

Measure the concentration of NO_2 and try to reduce it to zero by changing water in order to remove excretory products. The best condition is to have no nitrites. This may be possible by changing the water while siphoning off excretion and uneaten food daily. Change one-third to one-half of the water each time. Now keep your own schedule consistent when you determine your own methods of raising fish.

Adulthood is reached when the discus are 12 cm or more. During this time you can see the results of your efforts. The blue stripes on the fish are clearer. The reason for the adult patterns is because of the proper raising methods and not because of heredity. If the body is high and the fish has large fins and a large body, your daily care was good.

The schedule for changing water for the growth periods in a 90 to 120 cm aquarium is 20% to 30% every 3 to 7 days. You can't change the blue color or patterns of the fish any longer at this time. If you change the water for a large beautiful color discus too often, it loses its intense color and the skin gets soft. Therefore, you better change the water less often during this period.

During this period the adult fish becomes sexually active and you may wind up with a mated pair.

So the people who get beautiful pairs are the champions of changing water and proper daily care.

There are two kinds of water to use. The first is tap water and the second is well water. If you use well water, you will have to let it sit for at least 24 hours before using. I cannot say which is better but in my opinion tap water can be good or bad depending upon your location and the time of the year. For example, in Hokkaido or in Kansi, water from the tap is always the same so it is no problem in these areas. But in Kantou, Tokyo, water comes from many different reservoirs at the same time so it is possible that the water quality is not always the same. So in this area you should use well water. Even when you use well water you should make sure the water is always the same by using test kits and water conditioners.

In trying to manage the water, you should use such water conditioners such as zeolites, peat moss, and activated carbon. These we will talk about more later on.

TEMPERATURE

Water temperatures for discus are basically better when kept slightly high. Especially during their early stages, 32°C is good. But as they grow, the temperature can be gradually lowered to 27-30°C.

Igarapes and small streams associated with the Amazon from which the original discus come have temperatures of 26° to 28°C.

People say there are low temperature areas of around 20 to 24°C, but when the raising water temperature is below 24°C the discus body condition changes and their color gets dark and they lose their appetite. So although raising discus at 25 to 26°C is

Various pumps and filters are available for every size tank and every step of discus raising. The equipment should match the job it is to do. Seek advice from your supplier if necessary.

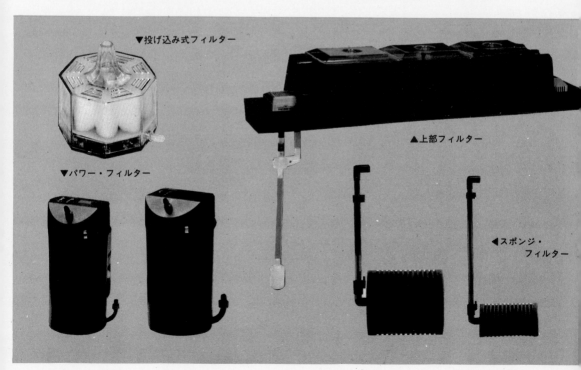

▼投げ込み式フィルター

▲上部フィルター

▼パワー・フィルター

◀スポンジ・
フィルター

okay, we think the best temperatures are 27 to 30°C.

Let's talk about maintaining the temperature. As long as the discus is provided with the necessary equipment to grow, the heater (especially one with a good thermostat) then becomes the heart of the raising equipment. But you cannot trust it 100%. Now I would like to introduce you to the thermal relay.

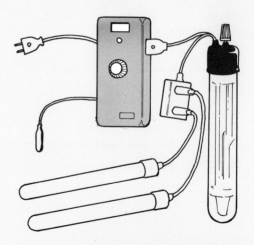

A diagram showing one type of set-up for heating aquariums. There are many different ways to do this, but make sure that your hook-up is both adequate for the task and safe.

Bimetal relays, such as this Japanese model shown here, are available in many well-equipped aquarium supply shops.

The relay type of temperature control is accomplished in the following way. Connect the heater to the bimetal thermal relay and set the heater thermostat to 28 to 30°C. Make the temperature 2 or 3 degrees higher than the bimetal thermal relay. In this way, even if the bimetal thermal relay burns up, the water temperature goes up only 2 to 3 degrees and the electric thermostat helps to stop the heater.

On the other hand, to prevent the water from getting too cold, you can use two heaters. For example, instead of using one 150 watt heater for a 60 cm aquarium, you can use two heaters, one 100 watt and one 60 watt. For a 75 to 90 cm aquarium, use two 100 watt heaters instead of one 200 watt heater. In this way you will still have one operating to prevent a sudden drop in temperature in case the other stops working.

DIFFERENT KINDS OF FOOD AND HOW TO FEED THEM

The food that influences the body shape and color is as important as the ideal water conditions.

DISCUS "HAMBURGER"

Discus "hamburger" is a frozen food that has beefheart as its main ingredient and is the best discus food you can get. You just feed it once or twice a day. One portion for two adults or one portion for five juveniles should be sufficient. For the juveniles you might have to shave it to make it easier for the fish to eat. It is a food I recommend because it has the ability to enhance the color. Wild discus do not eat it alone, so mix this with other foods and let them get used to it. When you make homemade "hamburger" do not add any unnecessary food or too much of anything but carefully measure the ingredients.

LIVE FOODS

Bloodworms and water fleas are sold in pet shops. Discus love live foods. Try and feed live foods once every day or at least once every other day. Some people say viral diseases and parasites can be traced to these foods, but don't worry about this. It is a fact that many people are feeding their discus these foods without such problems. I personally recommend bloodworms and other insects.

DRIED KRILL AND FROZEN MYSID SHRIMP

To keep the red color of discus, including the Red Royal Blue Discus from Southeast Asia, we must supply the fish with food that contains lots of carotene, like krill and mysid shrimp. Moreover, these foods are easy to get and the discus like to eat them. Baby fish can eat them also if you shred them first. Also, lobster eggs have the same effect on the color, but they are expensive.

You have to change water very often because leftover foods can foul the water faster than usual.

DRY FLAKE FOOD

Flake foods are also favorites once the discus get used to them. There are some flake or dried foods made especially for discus that have good nutritional value, and we can even use them as a side dish.

CHECKPOINTS BEFORE OR AFTER YOU BUY THE FISH

SELECTING THE FISH

The most important thing when you buy a fish is to make sure it is a strong, healthy fish. Discus are imported in small plastic bags without food for several days. So it is basically a strong fish. The discus may not die in such a situation, but they are weakened. It is true that there are also some fish that arrive with damaged fins. The point is to select the ones that recover soonest and start eating right away.

Avoid the ones that are breathing too fast as they might have parasites that will cause the fish to become easily exhausted. The strong fish that have strong fins and could damage these sick fish will have no problems.

Look at the shape of the body. Inbred strains from bad parents or baby fish raised in bad water can produce oddly shaped fish. Fish with twisted fins, poor gill structure, and oddly shaped faces are the ones we want to avoid. When the fish swims abnormally, or when it's darker than normal, you shouldn't buy it unless you have the confidence and ability to raise it.

After all, you have a good choice through experience of looking at many fish.

MEDICINAL BATHS FOR YOUR DISCUS

Discus can change their body conditions even if they are not sick because their way of feeding is different from that of other fishes. One disease that is hard to cure is skin disease. A sign of the disease is that the edges of the fins become white and disappear (like tail rot disease). When it becomes worse, the skin becomes red and raw. The fish become dark and some swim oddly. This disease occurs primarily in Red Discus and Red Royal Blue Discus.

The treatment for this disease is to raise the temperature to 35°C. For example, giving a bath for 3 hours in one-half the regular amount of water can cure the disease when it first starts.

If it is not completely cured, repeat the treatment after 3 to 4 days. It is better to keep the water temperature slightly higher until the fish are completely cured.

Because of the treatment, sometimes the body color changes. However, in two weeks it will return to normal. There are some discus that also have trouble with their senses (orientation) because of the medication. After you cure the fish, you will have to watch the fish closely.

Parasites on the gills are a problem we cannot avoid when we raise discus. For parasitic infestations we can use formalin. A concentration of 1 cc of formalin per 10 liters of water is recommended. Therefore, for a 60 x 30 x 30 aquarium use 15 to 17 cc of formalin. After 3 hours in this bath, change 5/6 to all of the water. For some fish even this concentration of formalin is too strong, so watch the fish while it is in the bath. If you see the fish lying down, don't keep it in the bath for the full 3 hours. Change the water sooner.

For baby fish, when the condition of the gills is worse, they might die in 3 to 4 days. Presume that they had parasites when you bought them and give them a prophylactic formalin bath. Then you can raise them with other fish without any problems. Their appetite will return after the medicinal bath.

When you see a fish only occasionally rubbing lightly against objects in the aquarium, use about one-fifth the normal quantity of malachite green.

BASICS OF BREEDING

It is well known by many people that some tropical fishes have the habit of taking care of their fry. Among them the discus has the unique ability to secrete a substance from the skin of the body that is of nutritional value to the fry.

Several years ago all of the breeding was done by professional breeders. Today, however, data is being gathered by the hobbyists around the country who want to try and breed the discus. Brown, Red, Turquoise, etc., are basically similar when dealing with the methods of breeding discus. In this section I want to introduce you step by step to the methods that are used today.

RAISE A GOOD PAIR OF PARENTS FOR BREEDING

To obtain a good pair of discus for breeding you have to raise the pair yourself. There are some people who start their breeding program with a pair of adults. But you will be more successful if you start by raising your own fish instead of buying adults because through your daily care of the babies you will get to know the characteristics and personality of each fish. This way you will get pairs naturally, so this method has many good points. Also, the price you will have to pay for a pair of adult discus would buy many babies.

Raising baby discus requires only keeping the water clean by making water changes 1 to 3 times a day and feeding mainly discus "hamburger" and live foods such as bloodworms, river worms, etc., along with some dry or frozen

繁殖の基本

foods. This is not so easy, but only conscientious daily care will be the fastest and most successful way to breed and raise discus.

I also want you to enjoy watching the development of the colors as well as to have the satisfaction of raising them into strong, healthy fish.

After 3 to 5 months, when the fish have grown to 6 to 7 cm, they will have reached sexual maturity and start pairing off for mating. Until the fish reach 10 cm or more, you should continue the same feeding and water changing schedule.

It is important that the fish get used to people during this time and not be frightened at every little sound. Also try and make them understand that you will not harm them and that you are the one who gives them their daily care. This way you may help prevent the parents from eating their own eggs after laying them or becoming frightened of sounds and causing or incurring injury while they are taking care of the eggs and baby fish.

If they get used to people, they will not fret so much when you have to change the water in the breeding tank.

To get mated pairs, it is easiest to start with 5 to 10 fish 10 cm in size in a 75 to 120 cm aquarium. As the pairs are formed one by one separate them out.

Place the spawning substrate into the aquarium. This will excite them into laying eggs. Some will even lay eggs on the glass or the plumbing of the pump or filter even if you do not place anything in the tank upon which they can lay their eggs.

In the aquarium, the female sometimes attempts to choose a territory, but usually the strongest male will choose both the territory and the female. When another male fish comes too close to the spawning substrate the stronger male will drive away the weaker one. But when a female comes close he will try and attract her.

At this time you should decrease the quantity and frequency of the water changes, although this will depend on how dirty is the water. Change 25% to 33% of the water every 3 to 4 days. By decreasing the water changes, the fish will be stimulated to spawn.

In the meantime, a male and a female who look like they might be a pair are no doubt closely eyeing the spawning substrate.

It is difficult to tell males from females, but by following the points noted in the diagram you should have a fairly good chance to distinguish one from the other.

Especially in the Turquoise Discus, there are many females with much more beautiful shapes than the males. Please use your own judgment and methods to select and separate them.

Keep the fish under observation for several days once you notice them pairing off. They will behave like a mated pair once they have settled down. At this point in time you should move them to the breeding aquarium. If you move the dominant pair from the holding aquarium to the breeding aquarium, the next dominant male will start the whole process all over again, and so on.

I want you to try and distinguish the males from the females.

SETTING UP THE BREEDING AQUARIUM

For pairs about 14 to 15 cm, you can use a 45 x 45 x 45 cm or a 50 x 50 x 50 cm tank. But the best is a 60 x 45 x 45 cm aquarium. The 45 x 45 x 45 cm aquariums are the ones normally sold in Japan but they are not popular so it may be better

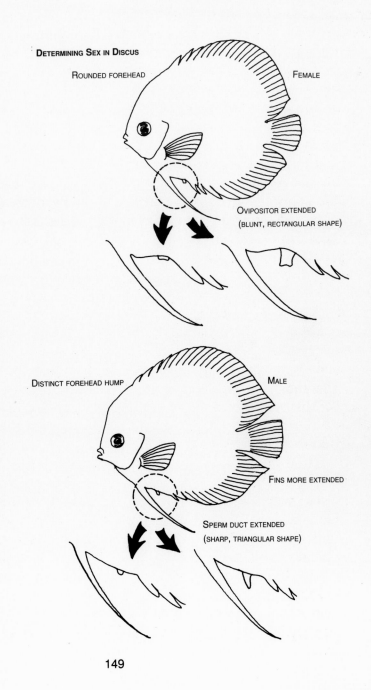

DETERMINING SEX IN DISCUS

ROUNDED FOREHEAD

FEMALE

OVIPOSITOR EXTENDED
(BLUNT, RECTANGULAR SHAPE)

DISTINCT FOREHEAD HUMP

MALE

FINS MORE EXTENDED

SPERM DUCT EXTENDED
(SHARP, TRIANGULAR SHAPE)

to have one custom-made.

When considering spawning and water changes after hatching, the feeding of the fry, etc., you will think that an aquarium of 75 to 90 cm is too large. It is possible to use the 50 cm aquarium but it is very difficult to maintain the water quality. Plan on spending about 20,000 yen ($160) if you are trying to breed the King of Tropical Fishes, the discus. If you buy two or three tanks at one time, you might be able to get a discount.

You have to try not to make the stream of water from the filter too strong because, generally, discus only give off a few sperm and are not proficient at fertilizing the eggs. The male that has a strong breeding ability can fertilize eggs in spite of the water flow from the top filter but for many males the strong water flow is not good.

I am sorry to say that there is no filter available with a low water flow and a high filter capacity combined. We have to try to use the filters available and modify them. Considering the 60 x 45 x 45 cm aquarium as a standard size, please use a 60 cm top filter, which is sold as a main filter with the water pump having lots of power. You have to adjust the stream of water so that it is not so strong.

There is a way to make the intake water less by winding a sponge and filter wool around the strainer. There is also a way using a river worm case and an egglaying box as a dish under the stream to diffuse it. Using them as upper filter will work as a main filter of the breeding aquarium of discus.

For substrate filters use a sponge filter like a BRILLIANT filter, which is very convenient. It has a high filtration capacity and it can filter out visible dust and excrement in spite of its appearance. This filter is better than other filters near the point of the egglaying substrate and the fry gathered around the parents are not sucked in. Recently, there have been several other types with different water quantities available. For the 60 x 45 x 45 cm aquarium the BRILLIANT Double and the BRILLIANT Super filters are the best.

It is common to use sponge filters connected to air stones, but remember to use only the sponge part. Put this sponge in the intake of the power filter. In this way you can maintain the water quality by the filter medium that is in the power filter (use peat and activated charcoal) and there is no danger of the fry being sucked in.

You can try this with the outside filter and the substrate filter.

The best temperature for spawning discus is 27° to 28° C. Basically, the raising temperature is 30° C, but this is too high for breeding. When the temperature is too high there is normal spawning but very often the eggs do not hatch and the parents eat the eggs. For the brown discus there is little problem, but for the RRB and the Turquoise this 2-3° gap is very important. The same goes for the water quality. I want you to measure the 27° or 28°C temperatures correctly by using good quality thermometer because there are lots of different kinds on the market and some are far from accurate.

WATER QUALITY

If the discus pair lays eggs and we take the fry from the aquarium to raise them, there is nothing easier than this. But the "king of tropical fishes" doesn't do things our way. Most of the reasons for this are due to water quality.

The pH should be 5.5 to 6.5. I know that the ideal carbonate hardness should be 0°DH. The hobbyists who have not measured these parameters and do not know how to take care of any adjustments needed are the ones who must learn the step-by-step methods before they can have any success with breeding fishes.

I want you to get a pH meter and a test kit to measure KH and GH. Read the instructions carefully.

Recently in and around the big cities the supply of drinking water from a single source is decreasing. Waters from several sources are now blended, especially around Tokyo, and the quality of water is not stable throughout the year.

We are required to think that the quality of water is the most important factor in raising discus.

You might notice the differences over a three-day period—just after changing the water, after 6 hours, after 24 hours, after 48 hours, and after 72 hours. Those people who think that the pH will remain at 6.0 to 6.5 after three days without changing water will be surprised. Except for areas like Kansai in Tokyo, the water doesn't exhibit acidity (low pH) very frequently.

As it happens, because of the chemicals added to the city water, we have to reduce or remove them by putting peat moss or zeolite in the filter or by using chemicals to lower the pH.

Chemicals are available on the market to adjust the pH. Some of these are very easy to use. For example, a capful of one leading brand can reduce the pH about 0.5 in a 60 x 45 x 45 cm aquarium. You should use these every time you change the water since it doesn't take long to accomplish and to test the water afterward.

Change one-third to one-half of the water once a day. Try to maintain the pH at 6.0 to 6.5. Before you get used to using the chemicals, try using them little by little until you can get the hang of it.

Talking about the hardness, this is the numerical value that shows the quantity of carbonates that are combined with calcium and magnesium. The point is to reduce the mineralization. This is easy and fast using an ion exchange resin. One drawback is that it is not easy to find resins in aquarium shops, but nowadays more and more pet shops are carrying them.

When you can manage the quality of the water, success with breeding is just around the corner.

EGGLAYING

When all the conditions are right, the mated pairs will start to spawn. This is what we are looking for. During this time you have to be patient. Although you may be very pleased with the spawning of your discus, you still have to keep in mind the management problems that will arise after the egglaying. It is important not to stimulate the parents, especially the male, during this season. The younger the parents, the more space for spawning and egglaying is needed and the less possibility there is for fertilization. But after several attempts at egglaying, you will see 200 to 400 eggs adhering close together in an area of 3 cm x 6 cm to 8cm.

Breeding success differs from pair to pair. Some pairs will succeed in spawning the first time while others may not succeed until the tenth try. The smaller female, which is about 12 cm, has better possibilities to be a good breeder than the larger size female of about 15 cm. The larger the fish grows the more likely it will have a tendency to become neutral sexually. It will fight with the males and will not care for the eggs after they are laid.

After spawning, good pairs cooperate with each other and take turns fanning the eggs with their pectoral fins in order to keep dirt off them. They also use their mouth in cleaning the eggs. If they behave in this manner keep the lights on all day and all night because sudden brightness or darkness may trigger the parents to eat the eggs. A light of 15 to 20 watts is sufficient.

You can feed the parents as usual after egglaying, but keep the water quality the same as that at the time of spawning. You better feed live foods like bloodworms and tubifex as they are better than the high protein prepared foods like the "hamburger."

Two days after the eggs are laid the body color of the parent discus starts to change—this is the first sign of discus milk secretion.

HATCHING AND RAISING BABY DISCUS

At a water temperature of 28°C, hatching starts about 60 to 72 hours after the eggs are laid. Just before hatching, the color of the eggs changes from light brown to dark brown. When they start to hatch, the fry are watched carefully by the parents and often they will be carried in a parent's mouth to another site.

The fry will adhere tightly to the spawning substrate by the threads attached to their heads. Fry of 7 mm do not have any eyes yet. It is desirable that they "swim" well at this time (make strong tail movements). We can think of ways to make them do this. When the fish are not healthy at this stage, due to the deterioration of the water, the tail may be warped. This is hard on these fish.

This is the most difficult and most important time for the fry. Try changing water, from 20% to

33%, even if it is just before hatching time, if the water looks bad.

Sometimes we need the courage to change the water. Although we would like to change the water, we might hesitate, thinking that the parents might eat the eggs or fry. The parent fish that were themselves raised since they were fry are not often disappointing as breeders.

The baby fish soon develop eyes and the fins grow. They become more active and feed but the thread is troublesome. They are not comfortable with the thread. At this time 5 to 10 fish may even get tangled together in their threads.

When the baby fish leave the breeding substrate, they will quickly be returned because of their being carried back to the group of fry in a parent's mouth. They are able to start swimming freely one to two days after this.

The fry that have the ability to swim freely start feeding on the discus milk by contacting their parents' bodies. You can be sure the fry are growing by observing them every day. They will soon become discus shaped like their parents.

Be sure to change water properly from this time for up to one week after hatching. Feed them with baby brine shrimp 5 to 6 days after they start feeding off their parents.

In spite of the fact that they are absorbed in eating the discus milk from their parents and apparently ignoring the brine shrimp, one by one they will start eating the baby brine shrimp. You can tell if they are feeding on the brine shrimp by

Electron scanning micrograph of head of larval discus showing the three pairs of adhesive glands.

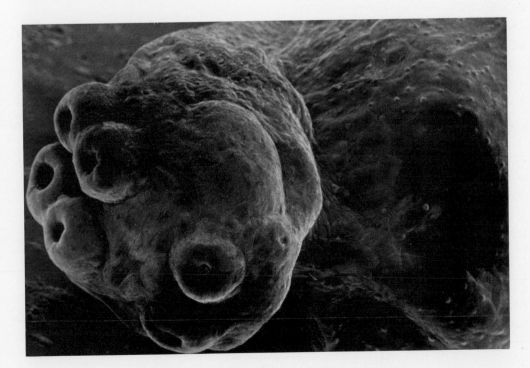

looking at their stomachs. By eating the brine shrimp the baby discus's stomach will take on an orange color. The ones that only eat the discus milk will still have a gray-colored stomach. At this time you have to make sure that all of the individual fry eat every 1 to 2 hours.

You must feed them at least twice a day, although feeding every two hours is preferred. This will keep you busy hatching baby brine shrimp. Brine shrimp eggs these days have a high percentage of hatching and are also becoming less expensive. It's good to hatch a lot.

After feeding the baby discus with baby brine shrimp, change water once or twice a day to remove the uneaten shrimp. Because the leftover brine shrimp, which are crustaceans, will cause the nitrites to become very high and eventually cause the death of the fry, change 50% to 100% of the water every day.

Two weeks after hatching, or from the time the parents dislike the fry contacting their sides, it's time to separate them. At this time the baby discus have grown to a size of about 1.5 to 2.0 cm, and they are able to eat discus "hamburger" or tubifex. Separate the pairs that have finished raising their fry to the 75 to 90 cm aquariums, using separators, and give them a rest.

Just after separating the parents from the baby fish, both the male and the female become rough. Some of them lay eggs soon again, but most of them just become offensive. You should try and let the adult fish recover their strength.

A few days after separation, let the pairs that recover by eating sufficient food lay eggs in the aquarium again. The original fry should be 4 to 5 cm by now.

There is a lot of fighting between the pairs after the spawning because sometimes one of the parents may try to monopolize the fry. In this instance, it is a good idea to separate the parents and allow one of them to raise the fry alone.

You need a technique for breeding by selecting a specific male and female. The most important thing for discus breeders to remember is to watch their discus day after day.

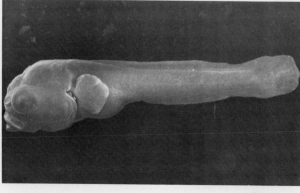

A 6-day-old discus fry. The eyes and mouth are well developed while the fins still have a ways to go.

稚魚育成の秘訣はこれだ

筆 秀一

PROFESSIONAL BREEDER'S DISCUS BREEDING METHODS

THE SECRET OF RAISING YOUNG DISCUS

BY SHUICHI FUDE

When I started working with discus about 10 years ago, the breeding of discus, even the satisfactory raising of the young to an adult stage, was very difficult. Of course, homebred or domestically produced discus were not available and the condition of young fish (imported only in small quantities) was poor. For this reason, the purchase of a group of young fish was difficult and the price was several times more expensive than it is now. It was a time when there weren't any established methods for breeding them and no good instruction books.

After many years of trial and error, I invented a new method of breeding discus and had it published in a technical magazine. I took the discus's natural behavior into consideration, calculated what is favorable to the discus and, on the other hand, what is favorable to the breeder, with the result being a healthy growing discus well accustomed to people.

With the release of my method, breeding discus has rapidly grown easier in the past few years, making it possible to produce healthy adult breeders. Many successful breeding stories, which were not imaginable 10 years ago, are now heard of. In this article, I would like to introduce you to my breeding methods and talk about my experiences in which I daily observed the discus.

BREEDING PLAN

Some precautions must be taken if one is attempting to breed discus for the first time. Although the discus is timid, it has a habit of fighting with other discus. Therefore, it is wise to keep them at a uniform size and in large quantities. This is also important as a way to help them get used to people.

The number of discus to be kept in one aquarium should be enough even if it appears to be a little crowded. Obviously, water maintenance should be considered. This means that you should increase the frequency of water changes and make sure that the filter is always in good condition.

When purchasing the fish, don't be too particular about the different kinds at first. Instead, choose the ones that show no illnesses, that eat well, that do not have a blackish color, and that appear to be accustomed to people, and purchase as many as possible of uniform size within your budget.

Keep them at relatively high temperatures (about 33°C) at first, feeding them frequently and changing the water on a regular basis, gradually allowing them to grow accustomed to your tanks and your routine.

BREEDING METHOD WITH DIFFERENT SIZES AT THE TIME OF PURCHASE

–YOUNG FISH OF 3 TO 5 CM
  Except for the ones collected in the wild, this size of fish is widely distributed, the price is low, and breeding is easy. In general, the smaller the fish, the less it will be afraid of people, therefore becoming adapted more easily.

A 45 cm or 60 cm aquarium should be sufficient; there is no need to keep the fish in larger tanks from the beginning. The bigger the aquarium, the more fish will be needed to make them grow accustomed to people. For other reasons, diligent maintenance of a smaller aquarium will give better results.

The ideal number of 4-5 cm fish to be kept in a 45 cm aquarium is about 10; in a 60 cm aquarium about 10 to 15. A breeder who can change the water daily and give fresh live foods abundantly (I'll talk about food later) can keep up to 30 fish in the aquarium. To prevent weaker fish from dying one after another, also to prevent differences in size, which will definitely occur during the first year of breeding, it is better to keep more than 5 or 6 fish together.

Install only a thermostat and a heater in the aquarium; do not put any sand in the bottom. Be sure to use more than two inside type filters such as sponge filters. This is because when cleaning one filter the others can be kept in operation, preventing the decrease of filter bacteria which can spoil water quality. Clean the filter with aquarium water gently, not vigorously, under the faucet.

–HALF-GROWN FISH
OF 7-11 CM

Change to a 75 X 45 X 45 cm or a 90 X 45 X 45 cm aquarium and use an outside filter. In a 75 cm aquarium, keep more than 15 fish 6-11 cm in size and about 20 fish if they are 7-8 cm. I once kept 23 fish of 5-7 cm size, 15 of 7 cm size and 10 of 9 cm size, a total of 48 fish, in one 90 cm aquarium. I used both top and inside type filters.

Because there is no sand on the bottom of the aquarium, the reflected light on the glass will scare the fish and some will have problems getting accustomed. To avoid this, lay down a gray or white vinyl chloride sheet and also lay down a sponge sheet.

A 31°C water temperature is good for spawning, but about 30°C is said to be better for the fish "in heat."

The frequency of water changes depends on the size of the aquarium, the size and quantity of fish kept and the quantity and efficiency of the filters. I did as follows:

If using only the upper filter on a 75 cm aquarium, change 50-70% of the water once daily; if using both upper and inside filters, change 70% of the water once every three days; if using only the upper filter on a 90 cm aquarium, change 50% of the water every two days.

Use only fiber filtering materials in the outside filter, being careful not to cause any change in water quality with such things as feeding. Surprisingly, there are a lot of people who cannot properly maintain the outside filter. In the case of inside type filters, such as sponge filters, as long as there is no replacement with a brand new filter, water cloudiness resulting from over-cleaning (decrease of filter bacteria) is not very noticeable. Since discus breeding requires frequent water changes, it is said that there are also people who wash the entire amount of wool used in the outer filter. A tropical fish breeder may think this funny, but there are still a lot of people who believe that a filter is a cleaning device with the function of simply removing the waste in the water through the wool. I would like to remind you that what cleans the water is not so much the filter but the filter bacteria. This is not necessarily only the case in outside filters but can be said of all filtering methods.

–FULLY GROWN FISH OF MORE
THAN 11 CM

Once this far, special attention will not be needed and breeding will be a lot easier. Keep 5 to 15 fish in a 90 cm aquarium and feed them once a day. Changing 70 to 80% of the water about once every two days will be sufficient. But if you are using two outside filters and a power filter as well, changing about 70% of the water once a week is sufficient.

About now, some fish will be in heat so it is important to make sure all fish are well fed.

FILTERS AND FILTER BACTERIA

The most important thing in filter maintenance is to make sure there is no clog in the filter. In the course of daily maintenance, when the water looks cloudier than usual or the fish do not eat as much, there is a chance that the wool is clogged. Even when this happens, don't wash it entirely. Instead, gently wash only parts of it with aquarium water. This is to avoid a sudden decrease in the number of filter bacteria that were satisfactorily growing until then.

Since you cannot see the bacteria, always keep notes on the way the filter material is washed, how much of it, and the date/time. It is important for each breeder to learn the best cleaning method by experience. By continuing periodic maintenance throughout the year, you should be able to keep the fish in good condition.

While keeping discus, small white worms will sometimes appear on the sides of the aquarium. These worms will not cause any harm to the discus but their existence there is proof that the filter is not operating properly.

When the filter does not operate properly, the aquarium water will become cloudy (even if the water is changed daily) and the aquarium will become slimy. The "worms" favor this kind of environment and will reproduce inside the filter. In such cases, or when the filter material was over cleaned, use a filter bacteria starter or something that will help the function of the filter bacteria; these products are available at pet shops.

The interior of the outside filter consists of wool sheets and torn wool. The aquarium water is sucked up from the upper filter pump and falls on the entire surface of the wool through tube holes. In some outside filters sold in the market the water falls only in the middle of the wool, but in such a case just puncture the holes yourself.

Even if leftover food and feces are sucked up, they will be stopped at level (A). This part can be washed as often as wished. Because level (D) stops dead filter bacteria and fine waste, it can be used as an indicator for how clogged the filter has become. This part, too, can be entirely washed.

Levels (B) and (C) are the most important parts. They are not necessarily divided into two levels as in the picture. That's where you would want to have many aerobic bacteria growing. For this reason, instead of washing everything when cleaning, for example, you may only wash half of (B) and gently squeeze-wash (C) with aquarium water. Then lower (B) back into the filter and set (C) on top. The next time you clean, don't wash (C) and instead wash (B). Maintenance methods such as this should be learned by practice.

The standard condition of the filter is said to be better if the wool looks black with blackish brown water coming out when squeezed

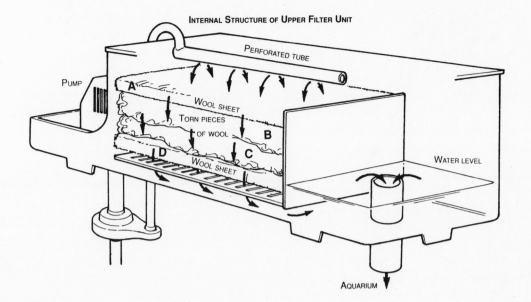

instead of white and fluffy. Be very careful not to over wash. By controlling this, there won't be any need to change the water that often and it'll be easier to raise the fish and have them reproduce. Therefore, do not neglect the water condition by rashly changing the filter material or the filter.

When using the outside filter, it is wise to use more than two at the same time to prevent a decrease in the bacteria and also for a better oxygen supply.

FOOD (FEEDING) TYPES

The most common live food is probably the bloodworm. Minced beefheart, tubificid worms, and artificially dried foods are also popular.

I'm often asked what is the best kind of food for discus. I say that when feeding one of the above foods alone, it may result in some difference in the discus's growth but not in their reproduction. Taking differences in cost, affect in water quality, and availability under consideration, it may be best to give a blend of foods.

–FRESH TUBIFICID WORMS AND BLOODWORMS

These are the favorites of the discus. Compared to other foods, they are the best because they grow rapidly and do not affect the water quality as much.

Unfortunately, their high cost, difficulty in preserving, and the fact that the discus will often not eat a different kind of food if their favorites are not available, cause a problem. Therefore, it is a good idea to have the fish accustomed to eating other kinds of food as an alternative in case fresh supplies are not available throughout the year or at least once a week.

–FROZEN BLOODWORMS

Give consideration when feeding these because the fish will not eat them as eagerly and the water will cloud faster compared to when giving them living food. Frozen food is preferred by many breeders because of its low cost and easiness to store. Growth will be faster when feeding abundantly. Check for freshness as the food will oxidize and become blackish in color and have a foul odor if it is stale. If possible, it is best to freeze them yourself.

–MINCED BEEFHEART.

This is also a breeder's favorite for its convenience in storing and choice of desired size for the fish, although a more frequent water change is required due to water cloudiness.

FISH WITH A SMALL APPETITE

There will always be one individual in the group that will not eat as well as the others. In the majority of cases this is not caused by an illness but by stress. Even when no signs of bullying are noticed, the weaker fish (blackish in color) is under some kind of stress, so increase the quantity of fish in the aquarium if there are not enough.

If this occurs even when there are enough fish in the tank or if you have increased their number, move the weak fish into a group of smaller fish where it stands in a more advantageous position.

As a last resort, the fish can be isolated. If you must do this, keep the water temperature around 35°C, dim the aquarium by wrapping sheets of newspaper around it, and give it smaller food items such as water fleas or beefheart, dropping them into the fish's view. Or give fresh food such as tubificid worms and bloodworms in the same manner. If the fish shows some interest or pecks at the food, it may recuperate, although slowly. If the problem is not discovered early enough, the fish may never recuperate.

Therefore, it is important to watch them closely when feeding them. No matter how hard you try to keep as many fish as possible in one small aquarium, there will always be some stronger ones keeping the weaker ones from getting to the food. For example, even after the food has sunk to the bottom of the aquarium, the stronger ones will guard the bottom area, not allowing other fish to approach.

As a way to prevent this from happening, the food could be collected again from the bottom with a net and dropped in once again or a gentle turbulence could be caused to drift the sunken food, allowing all fish to have their share.

IDEAL GROWTH RATE

There is no standard size when deciding if the fish is fully grown or if it is able to reproduce. In general, if the fish's metabolic activity is stimulated (by the quantity and frequency of water changes and feeding), growth will be faster. But, its size will not necessarily mean it has reached maturity and can spawn and reproduce.

Maturity and reproductive ability have more to do with age than size. To reach maturity, it takes a female from 1 to more than 1 1/2 years and it takes a male from 1 1/2 to more than 2 years. In general, a young fish measuring 4 to 5 cm at the time of purchase is about 4 months old or older. An experienced breeder or someone who knows about discus as much as professionals do may judge the age better by looking at the size of the fish's eyes and facial appearance than by looking at the fish's body size.

The criteria for age can be set as follows. At about 1 1/2 months of age the fish is about the size of 1" or 2 1/2 cm with a tail on it. When it's about 2 months old it's about the size of a 500 yen coin, up to 4 cm. However, those raised at a slower rate need 1 to 2 more months to reach this size. Those sold on the market are probably raised at such a rate. They need to have their growth stimulated right after purchase or they will end up being small parent fish. Even as they mature, there will be a great difference in the reproduction rate when compared with those raised getting plenty of nourishment (measuring about 20 cm). In general, the standard size of 3 to 4 cm fish after 6 months is 7 to 10 cm; after 10 months it is 10 to 12 cm; and after 12 months it is more than 12 cm. Naturally, if they grow faster, they will be less susceptible to diseases and their reproduction success will be higher, so it is better to raise them to be 14 to 18 cm in size by the end of one year and have them mate.

A fish that had a disorder during the course of development will naturally show poor development. Growth is especially slow in medium size fish that aren't very dominant or have a timid character, therefore not always able to get to the food. The ones that have only reached about 10 cm in size after one year and have eyes bigger than normal are useless for breeding purposes. Do not purchase older fish, although lower in cost, since they also are useless for this purpose.

FINDING THE RIGHT MATE

To form a pair, choose from the ones that are accustomed to people and grew up under favorable conditions. Except for older fish, which have experienced spawning many times, avoid those that have finally reached 15 cm in 3 years. These will not mate and, besides, it is difficult to find or choose a mate for them.

If possible, it is best to choose those you have raised from a young stage, with data on their growth process and habits.

A desirable size for the aquarium used for purposes of forming pairs may be 90 X 45 X 45 cm. A 60 X 45 X 45 cm aquarium or a 75 X 45 X 45 cm is good for breeding purposes but too small for forming pairs.

Don't start with only 4 or 5 fish but with 7 or 8 in one aquarium. This is important especially if the fish are relatively young, because the younger the breeding parents the more frightened they will be of a sudden change of environment, affecting their food intake. A large number of fish serves the purpose of inducing faster adaptation rather than forming pairs.

After a week or two, remove the ones that stay near the surface and those pushed into a corner. Also, remove those in bad condition right away. Finally, leave 4 or 5 fish (sometimes 3) together and observe them daily.

They will usually start by attacking each other indiscriminately, but soon there will be a particular one not attacked. Instead of waiting for a couple to exhibit closeness, judge their compatibility yourself. There will be some showing dominance

but no cooperation at all. In such cases, remove them or it as you would a weak one.

The principle of forming pairs is the opposite of when raising a young fish. It is better to break up the dominance balance.

DISCUS BEHAVIOR WHEN FORMING A PAIR

–FROM BODY DISPLAY TO BOWING MOTION

A discus behaves approximately as follows: First, there will be a competition for superiority. When this happens, the color of the eyes (red part around the pupils) and body will radiate more than usual. This is easily noticed if the fish is observed daily. At first it will

DOMINANCE AND AGGRESSION IN DISCUS

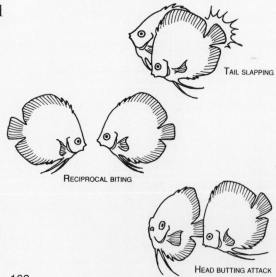

FINS FULLY SPREAD, BODY ANGLED

TAIL SLAPPING

RECIPROCAL BITING

HEAD BUTTING ATTACK

spread its fins to claim its territory. The discus will compete by facing and staring at each other, then, turning slightly sideways, threatening the opponent by spreading its fins (this is called body display). Next, the two fish may face or align themselves next to each other, swinging their tails against each other, emphasizing their strength. Another way is by biting each other's lips, both pulling and pushing. (This is a common behavior seen among other cichlids. It is said to be a way in which one fish checks the endurance of the other fish to be used in spawning. However, this is debated due to the fact that on occasion males will bite males and females will bite females.) In yet another way, a discus will thrust its head against its opponent.

By repeating these types of behavior, the weak and strong will be clearly decided. This is shown by the weak folding its fins and the strong spreading them, showing its dominance. This is how the ranking of the fish is determined and their territory claimed.

The weak and strong are distinguished not by their size or sex but rather by the state of sexual excitement and age. Also, the fish that came into heat the fastest or has been in heat longest is generally the strongest.

If a spawning substrate is put into the aquarium, the dominant fish in heat will claim the area around the substrate as its territory. As the state of sexual excitement develops within the dominant fish, it will begin to linger around the spawning substrate, guarding it. When other fish approach, the dominant fish will ward off the intruder by flaring its gills and using its body

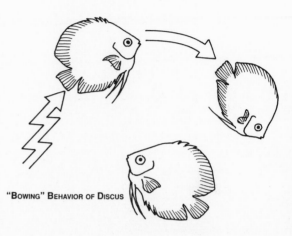

"Bowing" Behavior of Discus

to push the intruder away. When the state of excitement is at its highest point, it will begin quivering from head to tail. This is the time it will begin looking for a mate. This action can also be seen in an aquarium full of adult fish. Remember, these are the criteria to indicate when the discus is in heat.

If there are more than two fish behaving as said and attacking one another, remove one of them from the aquarium. Allow the one remaining (whether male or female) to lure its mate. Since the dominant fish will not leave its area around the spawning substrate, it will either lure or repel the approaching fish. When the mate is determined, the dominant fish will flare its fins and swim upward, canted, in a zig-zag pattern and will then close its fins as it descends. I call this activity "bowing."

If the other fish is also in heat, it will then respond to the bowing; if not, it will ignore the signals. When this happens the dominant fish will try to stimulate a response using the intimidation technique discussed earlier or will lure another mate. The behavior of persistent thrusting of the head against the other's abdominal area seen in other fish species has the purpose of stimulating spawning after the couple is formed in the case of the discus.

–POINTS TO REMEMBER WHEN PAIRS ARE FORMED

Pairs formed in such a manner will still fight at times, but as long as they are exchanging courtship behavior they should stay together. Even after a pair is successfully formed and only they remain in the aquarium, the younger the couple are, the greater the chances of a breakup. For instance, even if the female has spawned, if the male does not fertilize the eggs there will be a furious fight between them. If this happens, add another weaker fish to the aquarium and observe the developments. If this fails it will be better to change the pair's arrangement.

I leave a dim light on besides the lighting used during the day from the time the pairs formed, allowing them to adapt to the dim night lighting and making it easier for them to protect the eggs after spawning takes place.

The dim light is enough for the discus to slightly see each other and at the same time it allows us to observe the aquarium, the spawning substrate, and the fish. When observing a couple pairing under these conditions, you might be surprised to find a few compatible ones.

A good pair does not necessarily mean that one is a male and the other a female. Some fish may just get along well with others. Anyway, move them from the pairing aquarium to the breeding aquarium.

When two fish exchange courtship by putting their heads up high, spawning will take place relatively soon. And, when this pair attacks other fish to secure a territory, a second pair will usually form out of the remaining fish. After this, you may either wait for a third pair to form from the three remaining fish or add two more potential mates to the aquarium. Continue forming pairs in this manner.

–MEASURES TO BE TAKEN WHEN SPAWNING OCCURS

In a case when many pairs have formed, the first pair formed will not necessarily spawn first. There are many cases in which nothing happens after the pairing takes place or, when pairs appear to be compatible and are always preparing the spawning substrate by cleaning it, but again, nothing else happens. First of all, pairs are easily formed only by putting some adult fish together. I think that nowadays, behind one pair that succeeded in reproducing there are 1000 pairs that failed.

Sometimes this wall can be easily broken down and sometimes not. It is not rare to see cases in which a pair will remain together for many months or years after the spawning has taken place without any further development or spawning has not taken place but the pair remained together. In the long run, it is not unusual to find that only a few will succeed in reproducing.

I would like to introduce a few points and measures for breaking down that wall by taking the fish's behavior into consideration.

-METHODS FOR COPING WITH NON-SPAWNING FISH

- IS THE SPAWNING FISH TOO YOUNG?

If this is the case and the pair is far enough into heat to be preparing the spawning substrate frequently, then try adding a smaller and weaker fish to help accelerate the heat stage. However, there are cases in which one fish may be preparing the spawning substrate while the other is inattentive. In such cases, the inattentive fish may be too young and needs to be replaced.

- IS THERE TOO MUCH LIGHT?

If you think there is too much light to promote spawning, try dimming the lights and/or putting a skirt around the aquarium.

- COULD THE PAIR BE RESTLESS?

Discus will begin to spawn 2-4 hours before lights are turned off. Therefore, change the water in the morning instead of the evening.

When turning the lights on and off on a day-to-day basis, try to keep the time difference within one hour.

- IS THERE A LACK OF STIMULATION OR OPPORTUNITY?

Try to cut the intake of food by more than one-half. If the pair has been preparing the spawning substrate periodically, and then increases vigorously, stop feeding the pair for two to three days.

- IS THERE A PROBLEM WITH THEIR FEEDING?

Check the female to see if she has been over- or undereating. If this is happening, adjust the amount of intake to bring it to the ideal condition.

If the fish seems fat, postpone the spawning, then increase the amount of food given. Also, change water more frequently. Whether the food intake was too much or too little, it will take 1-2 months for an adjustment.

- IS THE AQUARIUM CONDITION SUITABLE?

Height is more important than the bottom area. The water level has to be about 40 cm high. Since light will affect spawning and is also important when the parent fish protects their eggs, try to move the spawning substrate around the aquarium to find the most suitable place to set it.

- WHAT IS THE CONDITION OF THE SPAWNING SUBSTRATE?

The condition of the spawning substrate will naturally depend on water quality. Substrates made from bricks or ceramic, which are sold on the market, will sometimes produce lye, greatly affecting the water. Repeatedly wash a brand new spawning substrate and soak it in water for a long time before using it. Used ones should be treated in the same manner before reusing.

-COPING IN CASES IN WHICH ONE OF THE PARENTS EATS THE SPAWNED EGGS

- IT IS POSSIBLE THAT THE MALE DISCUS MAY BE TOO YOUNG.

This happens when the male eats the eggs as soon as they are spawned or waits until after some fungi have formed on the eggs. The latter example is more common. When asked for advice, I used to say that this may happen when pairs do not get along, but after one year of further observation, I came to the conclusion that this happens when the male is too young. Since then, I've changed my advice by telling them to just wait, leaving all conditions unchanged. There have been many successful cases since then.

The discus's spawning period is from 5 to 10 times every 5 to 10 days (average of 7 days), resting for one to five months, and then repeating the process.

- IS THE BREEDER TOO ANXIOUS TO SUCCEED IN SPAWNING HIS FISH?

Lately, there have been many cases in which the breeder gets too anxious to succeed after a young pair has spawned, causing, instead, the pair to break up. Anticipation should be avoided. There are some pairs in my aquarium that have successfully completed the reproduction cycle and, although the spawning period is widely broken, some are still reproducing.

According to my data, reproduction is possible until an average of about 2 1/2 years after the first spawning and fertilization. Therefore, as long as the pair doesn't break up, reproduction is possible until about three years after the fish starts spawning.

As another example (although very rare), it could be possible that the pair is formed of two females. Also, it may be a case in which the pair simply get along, with only one of them spawning. In such cases try adding a smaller and weaker fish into the aquarium to help you judge.

-COPING WITH CASES IN WHICH THE YOUNG ARE EATEN AFTER HATCHING

- THE MALE DISCUS MAY BE TOO

YOUNG.

In such cases, patiently wait until he matures further and the fertilization rate increases.

- THE NUMBER OF EGGS HATCHED MAY BE TOO LOW.

In cases in which the number of hatched eggs is less than 30, some parents might eat their young. This is thought to occur when the parents assume their young to be too weak or when water quality is poor, causing low fertility rate. To prevent this from taking place, always keep the water clean, cut down the aeration during the spawning period, and set up the spawning substrate where the water is calm.

- THE FEMALE DISCUS MAY HAVE HAD POOR DEVELOPMENT OR IS IN BAD CONDITION.

In some cases the female may eat her young after they leave the spawning substrate. When this happens, the problem may be in the female herself as well as in water quality. One of the female's problems may be an unbalanced diet. Another one may be that the spawned eggs will hatch without producing any swimming young, the cause of which is unrelated to the male or water quality.

I separated the spawning substrate from the parents and conducted some experiments. I discovered that in some cases the egg cells did not multiply properly and in other cases the hatched young were not able to absorb the yolk sac, causing them to flip and fall off the spawning substrate. Actually, this happens to 1 or 2 out of 100 normally hatched young. From this, I came to the conclusion that the cause for the high percentage of deformed eggs lies in the female's poor physical development.

- COULD THE PARENT FISH HAVE A HABIT OF EATING THEIR EGGS?

In the case in which either the male or female parent eats its eggs or young, remove the one that eats them soon after spawning or hatching takes place. Although difficult, the remaining parent will raise its young on its own.

After the young fish has grown some, remove the parent less attached to the young in the case where the parents compete for their young. Or, caring for the young may go smoother when adding a weaker fish to the aquarium.

In cases where both parents have the habit of eating their eggs or young, try to have experienced, older parents to care for the young. Unfortunately, foster parents are hard to find because a fish normally does not care for another fish's young.

- COULD THERE BE A PROBLEM WITH FEEDING?

Especially in the case of young parents, some may eat their young when they are in the process of taking the nursing position (staying very near the parent's body) or after they have started to nurse. This happens when or if water quality becomes poor due to feeding or when the parents are so eager to eat that they will accidentally eat their young along with the food. Not feeding the parents from the time the young begin to swim until they are nursing or until one or two days after they begin to nurse may be a way to keep the parents from eating them. If the fish is healthy, there will not be any affect on the next spawning or on nursing if they are not fed for about 10 days. They will still be able to produce enough milk.

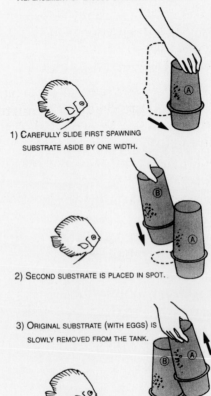

REPLACEMENT OF DISCUS SPAWNING SUBSTRATE

1) CAREFULLY SLIDE FIRST SPAWNING SUBSTRATE ASIDE BY ONE WIDTH.

2) SECOND SUBSTRATE IS PLACED IN SPOT.

3) ORIGINAL SUBSTRATE (WITH EGGS) IS SLOWLY REMOVED FROM THE TANK.

• COULD THE PARENTS BE TIMID?

A timid parent may eat its young from wariness caused by the breeder's constant observation or because of the aquarium lighting. If these are the cases, dissolve a small amount of methylene Blue (8 to 10 times weaker than when treating white spot disease) into the aquarium from the time of spawning until before the young separate from their parents.

Sometimes a few eggs may be dropped from the spawning substrate by the parents while they are protecting the eggs. Or, the parents may cause the eggs to fall when something startles them and the water is agitated. To avoid this, try covering the spawning substrate with a net.

-OTHER METHODS OF COPING (CHANGING THE SPAWNING SUBSTRATE)

If parents do not seem to be able to raise their young, try

168

exchanging the eggs you want hatched with the eggs of another pair that spawned during the same time by exchanging the entire spawning substrate.

The breeder must be experienced to do this because he will have to choose a substrate in which the eggs's location and appearance are similar, even scraping some off to arrange their number and shape. Also, the breeder should have many additional pairs spawning in order to match the exact spawning day for the exchange to be possible. Although it is important that the future foster parents are good, experienced parents, it may be a good idea to keep them trained.

In other words, train them to be used to having their spawning substrate picked up or moved by doing so from time to time.

This type of training may cause unnecessary excitement, so be very careful. The discus will eat their eggs if they feel they cannot protect them.

HOW TO PREPARE AND FEED BRINE SHRIMP

The young discus will grow by feeding on its parents's milk (body secretion), but in the cases where parents refuse to care for their young or when there is a need to separate the parents from their young, it becomes necessary to find another way to nurse them.

The brine shrimp, a staple diet of young tropical fishes, is also very important to the discus. Feed freshly hatched brine shrimp to the young discus.

How to Hatch Brine Shrimp

POLYEHTYLENE BOTTLE

WEAK AERATION

EMPTY JAR OR OTHER SUITABLE CONTAINER

THE EGGS MAY BE SCATTERED ON THE SURFACE AND ALLOWED TO FLOAT.

WHEN ONLY 0.5 GRAM OF BRINE SHRIMP EGGS ARE TO BE HATCHED, USE A WIDE-MOUTHED CONTAINER OR FLAT PAN. NO AERATION IS NECESSARY.

To hatch purchased brine shrimp eggs, put them in artificial salt water or make up a 3% salt solution. This is prepared by dissolving 12 g of table salt into 400 cc of water.

Pour the desired amount of brine shrimp eggs into the salt solution. Depending upon the origin of the eggs, they will start to hatch in about 36 hours at a temperature of 26° to 28°C or in about 24 hours at a temperature of 28° to 31°C. Most of them will be fully hatched after 5 to 8 hours.

Feed freshly hatched brine shrimp not only to young discus but to all young tropical fishes. As long as the salt solution is changed while it is still clean, the brine shrimp will live for about 2 days after hatching without getting any food.

If keeping only a small amount of brine shrimp, feed them small amounts of dried yeast dissolved in water. Be careful not to cloud the salt solution. If kept in this manner, the brine shrimp will grow to about 1 cm in three weeks.

You must make sure they are freshly hatched to feed to young discus. I keep about 5 to 6 bottles of brine shrimp available every day, preparing them by putting about 5 g brine shrimp eggs (up to 220,000 eggs per gram) in a 400 cc jar, thus making sure I always have fresh live food.

A young discus eats about 5 to 6 brine shrimp per second, therefore increase the amount to be hatched according to the quantity and size of the discus.

Separate the hatched brine shrimp and the eggshells because the latter are not good for the young fish. This can be done by siphoning out the brine shrimp 5 to 10 minutes after aeration has been stopped. Because the hatched

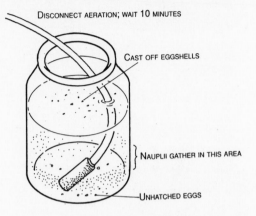

DISCONNECT AERATION; WAIT 10 MINUTES

CAST OFF EGGSHELLS

NAUPLII GATHER IN THIS AREA

UNHATCHED EGGS

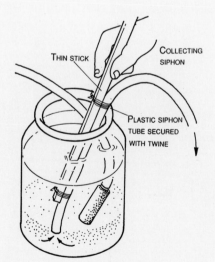

THIN STICK

COLLECTING SIPHON

PLASTIC SIPHON TUBE SECURED WITH TWINE

COLLECTING NEWLY HATCHED BRINE SHRIMP

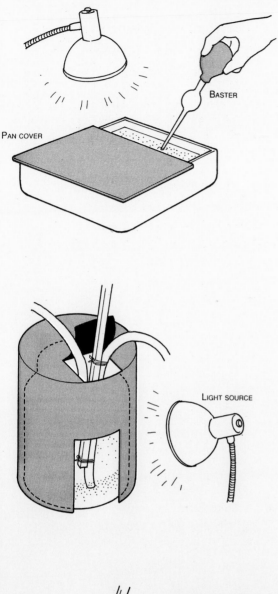

PAN COVER

BASTER

LIGHT SOURCE

brine shrimp are attracted to light, you can separate them from the shells. Small amounts of salt solution will not harm the young discus, but to be completely rid of it, filter the brine shrimp using a cotton cloth and wash them in fresh water before feeding.

I often hear about cases of unhatched brine shrimp eggs. Most times this happens if the eggs are old or there is a problem in preservation. When dry eggs get moistened or too much time has passed after their manufacturing date, they will never hatch or have a low hatching rate at times. Purchase them from reliable sources.

It is also not desirable to purchase more than the necessary amount just to take advantage of a bargain. When you have more than you need, try to preserve them by adding a drying agent or keeping them in a vacuum jar.

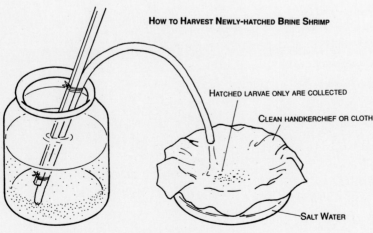

HOW TO HARVEST NEWLY-HATCHED BRINE SHRIMP

HATCHED LARVAE ONLY ARE COLLECTED

CLEAN HANDKERCHIEF OR CLOTH

SALT WATER

WHEN TO SEPARATE THE YOUNG DISCUS FROM THEIR PARENTS

Any breeder can easily raise a young discus after it has been with its parents for 1 1/2 to 2 months. Sometimes spawning will occur again about 10 days after the young discus begin nursing. When this happens, some parents may eat their young or their spawned eggs. At other times the parents may be too weak to care for their young, and there are also times when parents compete for their young, finally eating them.

A professional breeder may separate the young from the parents in order to expedite the next spawning. If there is enough time to spend feeding and changing the water, it's better to separate the young from the parents as soon as possible.

Except for the ones separated from the parents since their egg stage and artificially nursed, those young nursed by the parents for 7 to 10 days will safely grow on brine shrimp alone. They may be separated from the parents as early as 5 days after they begin nursing. However, the size of the freshly hatched brine shrimp fed to them must be very small (available in some areas).

Feed brine shrimp at least more than four times a day to young discus that were nursed for 7 to 15 days. The ideal amount of brine shrimp fed is when there are still a few left in the aquarium one hour after the feeding (brine shrimp will live for more than one hour in a 30° to 32°C water temperature). Drain the remaining brine shrimp and replace the water lost.

Feed 15- to 30-day-old young fish at least more than three times a day and 30- to 60-day-old fish more than twice a day. This frequency can be increased by three times if considering the discus's nighttime (when lights are out) to be 6 hours, and feeding them as often as possible during the remaining 18 hours. The growth rate of a discus raised under these conditions is astonishing.

There shouldn't be any problems raising them on brine shrimp alone, but because of its relatively high cost, it may be better to introduce other kinds of food and gradually change to them. Though these other kinds of food are lower in cost, they have a higher potential to cloud the water. Therefore, keep it in mind to maintain the aquarium cleanliness by changing water more frequently.

Start feeding brine shrimp before the young discus separate from their parents. Gently drop the brine shrimp near the young discus, being careful not to excite the parents. If the young discus's stomach area shows a reddish coloration, this mean that it has eaten the brine shrimp.

This process should be observed any time you change the type of food. Always gradually get the fish to grow familiar with the new taste and smell, mixing the new food with the one being fed before

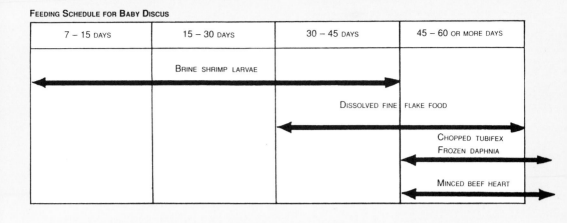

7 – 15 DAYS	15 – 30 DAYS	30 – 45 DAYS	45 – 60 OR MORE DAYS
	BRINE SHRIMP LARVAE		
		DISSOLVED FINE | FLAKE FOOD	
			CHOPPED TUBIFEX FROZEN DAPHNIA
			MINCED BEEF HEART

and never suddenly changing it completely. It's important to have the discus accustomed to eating a variety of foods selected by considering the discus bite size, the food's cost, and the frequency of water changes and of feeding.

HOW TO RAISE A DISCUS AFTER IT'S SEPARATED FROM THE PARENTS

Keep the young in a 45 cm or 60 cm aquarium. If only keeping 20 to 50 discus, a 30 cm aquarium should be sufficient.

Use a sponge filter that had been used on the same aquarium as the parents for more than one week prior to separation. Install it without washing.

Dim the lights and cover all sides except the front. Keep the water level at 20 to 25 cm depth to make it easier for them to feed on the brine shrimp. Keep the water temperature at 32°C to aid digestion.

Start the aquarium with 50% of the water from their parents's aquarium and 50% fresh water. After this, you may change 70-80% of the water later on. Death occurring during this time is caused more by poor water quality than pH or hardness level.

Try to scrub the aquarium walls with a sponge every time the water is changed. The secret to raising a healthy discus lies in a rich diet and frequent changes of water.

Although there are many success stories, there aren't many in which the discus grew larger than 2 or 3 cm. Even if some did reach 3 cm, they turned blackish in color and died. The cause of death in most of these cases was said to be a decline in appetite due to poor water quality rather than illness.

If you are not a professional breeder or do not have the time to closely watch the aquarium, it's better to increase the frequency of feeding during the time period spent caring for the fish (such as mornings and evenings) rather than to increase the amount of food given at each feeding. A very convenient method is to have a 75 cm or a 90 cm aquarium prepared aside, installing a sponge filter and maintaining aeration and filtering systems so as to always have extra water available.

DISEASES AND SYMPTOMS OF YOUNG DISCUS

• GILL DISEASE

It could be said that a young discus born to healthy parents and always kept in a clean aquarium is safe from any diseases for the period of time spent with the parents (until it reaches 3 cm at most). However, a problem exists if the parents have contracted gill disease. Because symptoms will not show, it is difficult to discover if the parents have already contracted the disease prior to or after spawning has taken place. If the fish is breathing faster and rubbing its gills against the spawning substrate, it means it's seriously infested with the parasites.

When a large number of parasites invade the young discus's gills, the fish will experience breathing problems, become blackish in color, will not eat well, and will rub its gills on objects in the aquarium. When keeping different sizes in the aquarium, only the smaller size fish will show some disorder in their breathing and behavior. The reason for this is thought to be because the younger the fish the finer its gill filaments are, and the easier for parasites to breed there.

In such cases, keep the young and adult fish together and add 2-3 cc of formalin solution (about 35% formaldehyde) to every 50 liters of aquarium water, changing more than 2/3 of the water after 4 hours. Repeat this treatment 3 times every 24 hours. Keep running the sponge and outside filters during the treatment.

This amount of formalin will usually not cause the total destruction of filter bacteria nor will it affect the young fish. While using any kind of chemical treatment, it is important to be able to keep a close watch. The chemical's effect on the fish or filters depends upon their condition. Therefore, always have some water prepared in case there is an adverse effect on the fish or water.

• FIN ROT DISEASE

The tail or fins of a young fish may become decayed through scratches after it has been separated from its parents. The discus will not scratch or split its fins as often as other fishes, therefore a young discus will not have split fins very often. However, if the fish only measure up to 1 cm after they've been separated from the parents, watch them for 48 hours. When putting them into a new aquarium, add 1 to 2 g of methylene blue to every 50 liters of aquarium water. After this, gradually bring the water back to normal by keeping up the water changes.

• DEATH CAUSED BY SWELLING OF ABDOMINAL AREA

This disease will not kill in great numbers. For instance, if there are 100 young fish in the aquarium, only 1 fish every 1-2 days will experience a swelling of the stomach and die. Do not be too concerned because as the fish grow the disease will disappear naturally and the loss will not be so great. If you are changing water right after feeding, it's better to raise the water temperature 1° or 2°C.

• PROBLEMS CAUSED BY SIZE DIFFERENCES

When raising the young discus away from the parents and a size difference is seen, separate the fish according to size, dividing them into two groups of large and small fish. Feed brine shrimp 2 to 3 times more often to the small size group for 7 days, bringing their sizes closer so that you are able to place them together in one aquarium again.

Above I have presented my own breeding method. I believe there is still room for improvement, but I am happy if I have been of any help to the readers.

Two tanks set up for raising young discus. The tanks are bare except for filters and a thermometer.

繁殖のポイントは
水質を自由に操ることだ

山田　洋

THE SECRET OF BREEDING IS TO CONTROL WATER QUALITY

by Hiroshi Yamada

Water quality is very important, determining life or death for the fish. Each kind of fish requires its own type of water. Also, there is a fixed range in the quality of the water. This is what allows a discus that lived in low acid water to live perfectly well in alkaline water. I call the range of water quality in which a certain fish can live "living water quality."

When a discus is kept in alkaline water, reproduction will not be successful no matter how much the effort. Even if the discus perform their dances and displays, proving a pair has been formed and also has shown spawning behavior, spawning will not take place. This is what water quality is all about.

Therefore, no matter how well they are paired and/or how good your breeding techniques are, if the water quality is not correct, you will not succeed. I call the range of water quality in which a

fish can breed "breeding water quality."

The figure demonstrates ranges in water quality. As you can clearly see, the breeding water quality is only a narrow portion within the range of the living water quality. This means that water used for reproduction purposes and the water used for

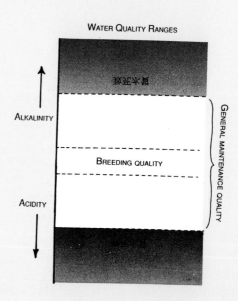

WATER QUALITY RANGES

ALKALINITY

ACIDITY

BREEDING QUALITY

GENERAL MAINTENANCE QUALITY

keeping purposes are not necessarily the same. In other words, if you intend to only keep the fish, you may use the full range of the living water quality and there are many keeping methods within this full range.

VARIOUS KEEPING METHODS
-KEEPING FISH IN ACID OR ALKALINE WATER

The discus can be kept in water quality ranging from slightly alkaline to acid water. Depending upon the individual, some may be kept in water as acid as pH 2.8. If the fish was kept in slightly alkaline or neutral water previously, however, it will not adapt to the sudden change and will not survive. It will survive only when its water quality is gradually changed to reach that level, allowing the discus to adapt.

In other words, the discus has the potential to adapt to this kind of change. While some aquarists prefer to keep the fish in acid water, some will prevent the water from becoming acid by using coral sand and/or oyster shells inside the filter system. The reason why two apparently opposite methods are possible is due to the discus' ability to adapt.

-RAINY AND DRY SEASON BREEDING METHODS

The basic method to breeding fish is to breed them in an environment as similar to their natural habitat as possible. In the case of the discus, I believe there

are two methods. These are the rainy season breeding method and the dry season breeding method.

In the Amazon, the continuous rain in the rainy season causes a regular change of the river water. Like the rainy season, the method

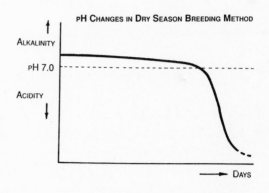

of changing large amounts of water every day is what I call the rainy season breeding method.

However, since there is a difference between the quality of water in the Amazon and the tap water used by us, the natural habitat cannot be exactly simulated.

Luckily, in Japan the tap water already has a low hardness, not becoming high in alkalinity even if used directly from the tap, thereby staying within the living water quality range.

Contrary to this method, the dry season of the Amazon does not allow much change in the water, the water remaining still, as in puddles and pools. What I describe as the dry season breeding method is a method in which water is not changed for a fixed period of time. This does not mean water can be left unchanged for about 6 months as in the Amazon. This is because there is a great difference in the volume of water per fish in the natural world versus that in an aquarium. The change of water quality occurring during the 6-month dry season period of the Amazon will occur in an extremely shorter period of time in an aquarium.

CHANGE OF WATER QUALITY IN AN AQUARIUM

Because of the large amounts of water being changed every day when using the rainy season method, there will not be a sudden change in the quality of the water. If there is a problem with the quality of the water, it lies with the tap water being used.

When using the dry season method, there will be a gradual change in the water quality since the same water is being used over a long period of time.

In the following, we will see how the water quality changes within the aquarium.

-WATER HARDNESS AND PH

When breeding fish, underground water is used in some areas but in most cases tap water is used. Water quality will be determined according to the amount of elements dissolved in the water, this, in turn, determining its pH and hardness.

Elements such as calcium, magnesium, potassium, and sodium are dissolved in water as chemical compounds and positive ions. Let's discuss calcium and magnesium, which have important effects on living things. Hardness of the water describes how much of these elements is dissolved in the water as calcium oxide and magnesium oxide.

In Germany and Japan, when 10 mg of calcium oxide is present in 1 liter of water, it is said to be 1 degree hardness (this formula is also used to measure magnesium oxide in the water). Usually, when the degree of hardness is above 20 the water is said to be hard, and if under 10 it is said to be soft.

Hardness is a problem in Europe because of the hardness of their water. But in Japan, for some reason, this is not the case. Even water that we consider to taste good has a high degree of hardness. Naturally, water used in large cities or suburbs with an established water system needs to be checked for hardness. However, even if underground water is available, it should be checked.

Checking the level of carbonate dissolved in the water is also an important indicator because in many cases carbonate is the element composing the hydrogen carbonate ion (also called bicarbonate ion). This is called carbonate hardness. The suitable carbonate hardness (in degrees) for fish breeding is said to be from 2 to 8. The bicarbonate ion has a lot to do with the pH.

The pH indicates whether the water quality is acid or alkaline.

This is determined (in theory) by counting how many grams of hydrogen ion (H^+) or hydroxyl ion (OH^-) are contained in 1 liter of water. Even in distilled water of neutral quality, a small part is ionized as $H_2O \rightarrow H^+ + OH^-$.

If there is a higher hydrogen ion concentration than this, the water will show acidity (pH value is lower) and there are more hydroxyl ions, the water will show alkalinity (pH value is higher).

The main elements that determine the pH value of tap and underground water are carbon dioxide and bicarbonate salts. Water with a lot of carbon dioxide will be acid, and that with a lot of bicarbonate salts will be alkaline. Normally, tap water will show a neutral quality even though containing such elements. Therefore, when using such water in an aquarium and carbon dioxide is removed through aeration, the alkaline bicarbonate salts will remain, thus causing the water to have an alkaline quality (pH 7.1-7.5).

-BUFFER ACTION

As discussed earlier, many chemical compounds are dissolved in the water, including H^+ and OH^-, with a pH value around 7 indicating it has a neutral quality. Even if elements containing H^+ or OH^- are mixed into the water, its pH will not suddenly change. This is due to the bicarbonate ion function. The reaction takes place as follows:

$$HCO_3^- + H^+ \rightarrow H_2O + CO_2$$

$$HCO_3^- + OH^- \rightarrow H_2O + CO_3^-$$

This means that, because the bicarbonate ion reacts with H^+, it can prevent a sudden increase of H^+ or OH^- concentration in the water.

This reaction in which the bicarbonate ion balances the pH of the water is what is called "buffering" action.

-CHANGE OF WATER QUALITY IN THE AQUARIUM

Even in Japan, where the water used has a neutral quality without any relative problems with water hardness and a sudden change in pH is prevented by the buffer action, a change in water quality will still occur during the process of breeding. This is caused by the nitrogen compounds (protein) contained in leftover food and waste from the fish.

As the nitrogen compounds decompose in the aquarium water, you'll find a build-up of ammonia (NH_3) or ammonium (NH_4^+), depending upon the pH. If the pH shows acidity, it produces a harmless ammonium, but if it shows alkalinity, ammonia will be dissolved in the water.

Since ammonia is very poisonous, be very careful if you keep your fish in alkaline water.

Ammonia will change to nitrous acid by reacting with the nitrous acid-forming bacteria, and also to nitric acid by reacting with the nitrate-forming bacteria.

$$N_2 \rightarrow NH_3 \rightarrow NO_2 \rightarrow NO_3$$

The nitric acid ion formed in such a manner will chemically react with calcium bicarbonate and magnesium bicarbonate in the water, finally becoming a nitrate such as calcium nitrate or magnesium nitrate. Nitrate has a neutral quality and will not cause any harm to the discus as long as its concentration is not too high.

However, this is true only if there is enough oxygen in the water and if the nitrous acid-forming bacteria and nitric acid-forming bacteria are denitrifying. When the amount of oxygen decreases, nitrification rate will slow and harmful ammonia and nitrous acid will linger in the aquarium. Also, the opposite of nitrification

$$(NO_3^- \xrightarrow{\circledR} NO_2^- \xrightarrow{\circledR} NO \xrightarrow{\circledR} N_2)$$

called denitrification will occur. In other words, a harmful nitrous acid will be formed.

Another fact to be careful with is a pH problem. Under normal filtration, as the amount of nitrates increase, bicarbonate salts in the water will gradually be consumed and finally disappear. This means that nitric acid will accumulate in the aquarium or, in other words, when there's no bicarbonate salts in the water, the pH will suddenly decrease.

ADJUSTING THE WATER QUALITY

-ADJUSTMENT BY WATER CHANGE

In the rainy season breeding method, in which large amounts of water are changed every day, we can say that the constant buffering action will keep the water from becoming acid. However, in the dry season breeding method, the water can suddenly become acid due to a reaction with nitric acid after a certain period of time. If you continue breeding under these conditions, the pH will keep decreasing, causing the acidity to be so high it will be way out of the living quality range.

In the case of discus, it is safe to assume that the lowest limit in pH of the living water quality is 4.5. When the pH is below 4.5 the cornea of the discus's eyes will be irritated by the acid and become cloudy. An especially weak discus will exhibit cloudiness in its eyes even at pH 5.0. Therefore, it is necessary to bring a decreasing pH back to neutral before it reaches the 4.5 level. If adjustment of pH is successful, the cloudiness of the cornea will clear in 1 to 2 days.

However, if adjustments are not made early enough, the acid will damage the inside of the eyes, resulting in blindness—even if the pH has been adjusted by then.

Compared to the rainy season breeding method, the dry season method takes a lot of burden off because of the fewer water changes, but, on the other hand, it has the disadvantage of having to deal with decreases in pH. Therefore, testing the pH level is a very important task when using this method.

Basically, if the pH is near 5.0 or 6.0, change the water. There is no need to change all the water, only half or a third is sufficient. By changing the water you are removing the acid contained and at the same time neutralizing that which remains. In other words, calcium bicarbonate contained in the new water neutralizes the acid that remained in the old water, decreasing its amount or entirely eliminating it.

The amount of acid decreased will depend on the carbonate hardness and the amount of water changed. If the carbonate hardness is high enough, its purpose will be served even with a small amount of water. Even the water in Japan, whose water hardness is considered low, should be changed by a third to a half. The only difference in the amount of water changed is that if the amount changed is small, the next change will have to be soon, and if the amount is large, the next change can wait a little longer.

-ADJUSTMENT BY CHEMICALS
• Adjustment by using coral sand and oyster shells.

Nitric acid accumulated in the aquarium water can be neutralized by a direct reaction with calcium carbonate, the main substance contained in coral sand, oyster shells, or bone powder. These can be put in the filter box when the pH needs to be adjusted, removing them as soon as the adjustment is made. The neutralization rate is relatively slow and differs with the amount of such substances as coral sand and the amount of water being filtered, but it should take from a half day to two days. The reaction takes place as follows:

$$CaCO_3 + 2HNO_3 \rightarrow Ca(NO_3)_2 + H_2O + CO_2$$

Carbon dioxide produced by this reaction can be removed through aeration and calcium nitrate will be removed when water is changed.

• USING SODIUM BICARBONATE
If you want to adjust the pH in a shorter period of time, use sodium bicarbonate. This is found in fire extinguishers, bleach, and used as baking soda. It is a substance obtained by changing the positive ion in the calcium bicarbonate (Ca_2^{++}) to sodium (Na^+).

Sodium bicarbonate is slow to dissolve in water but very convenient once you are used to using it. However, because it can cause too much of an increase in the pH if not used correctly, continuously test the water with a high accuracy pH meter.

Add small amounts of it while checking the pH meter. If too much is added, it will sink to the bottom without dissolving in the

181

water, so choose a place in the aquarium where it will easily dissolve and drop the powder there. Stop adding it when you reach pH 6.8-7.0. The reaction takes place as follows:

$$NaHCO_3 + HNO_3 \rightarrow NaNO_3 + H_2O + CO_2$$

Sodium nitrate produced by this reaction can be removed by water changes.

-MODIFIED DRY SEASON BREEDING METHOD

In the dry season breeding method, pH has to be tested from time to time and the troublesome neutralization task has to be performed. The modified version of this also allows the advantage of not having to change the water for a long period of time, but also saves the trouble of pH tests and neutralization. This can be possible by putting a small amount of coral sand or crushed oyster shells with the filter material beforehand, neutralizing the nitric acid by doing so.

Calcium carbonate contained in things such as oyster shells will not dissolve in the water by itself, but with the help of carbon dioxide (dissolved in the water or produced by the fish's breathing), it will become calcium bicarbonate, thus reacting with nitric acid.

This is the same kind of neutralization that occurred in the dry season breeding method:

$$CaCO_3 + CO_2 + H_2O \rightarrow Ca(HCO_3)_2$$

$$Ca(HCO_3)_2 + 2HNO_3 \rightarrow Ca(NO_3)_2 + 2H_2O + 2CO_2$$

However, while neutral or slightly acid water is used for the dry season breeding method, slightly alkaline water is used for the modified method. Calcium bicarbonate produced beforehand is of low alkalinity.

Since the coral sand is dissolved on a regular basis to produce calcium bicarbonate, check it every 3-4 months and add more if necessary.

However, when using the modified method, water must be changed periodically. The accumulation of calcium nitrate will increase water hardness and at the same time increase nitrate concentration. To remove it from the water, change about half the water at least once every 2-3 months.

The most important thing to remember when using this method is to keep the filters clean, which is easily forgotten since it doesn't require much water quality maintenance.

A dirty filter leads to poor water quality, which in turn can mean death to the fish. If the number of fish kept and the amount of feeding are both large, clean the filters once a month.

There is one big disadvantage to this method, this being that reproduction will not take place due to the pH being alkaline at all times. When coral sand or oyster shells are present in the aquarium, water pH is usually around 7.1-7.5. If not enough carbon dioxide is removed through aeration, the pH may go over 8 at times. Reproduction under these conditions is obviously impossible, but it will even be almost unsuitable to keep the fish.

When using this method, it is important to keep removing carbon dioxide through aeration to avoid an increase in the carbonate hardness and to keep the feeding regular to maintain a constant neutralization.

However, there are times reproduction is possible. But, in such cases, the filters were probably neglected and left to clog and neutralization was not taking place. In other words, dirt had covered the filter material or water was not flowing through the filter material, resulting in a pH decrease, making the water suitable for reproduction.

SUITABLE WATER QUALITY FOR THE DISCUS

In general, a suitable water quality for discus is low in hardness and contains no substances that can harm them. When pH or hardness is abnormally high and the water is full of impurities, we cannot say that that water is suitable.

Fortunately, the tap water in Japan is low in hardness and doesn't contain too many substances harmful to the discus,

therefore, suitable for breeding. However, it isn't always safe. Even the best of water will change during the process of breeding, for better or worse. In other words, even if the water is not very suitable for breeding discus, it can be improved during the process of breeding.

-RELATIONSHIP OF PH AND CARBONATE HARDNESS

If your goal is only to keep the discus and not to have them spawn, then you shouldn't have any problem as long as the pH of the water aerated in one day is between neutral and slightly alkaline. However, if the water shows acidity even after it has been aerated for one day, then you must keep changing the water and testing its pH diligently.

There is an interesting relationship between the pH and carbonate hardness in tap water. When breeding discus, there is no addition of carbon dioxide as in the balanced aquarium, and because water temperature is high (the higher the temperature, the less carbon dioxide will dissolve in water) the amount of carbon dioxide dissolved in the water is small, except in special cases. Therefore, the amount of carbonic acid formed in the water is also small.

The cause of acidity in the water is nitric acid formed from leftover food and waste from the fish. When nitric acid forms in the aquarium it will chemically react with carbonate and bicarbonate salts contained in the water, forming nitrates. The more nitric acid, the more carbonate and bicarbonate salts are consumed, causing a decrease in carbonate hardness. In other words, the carbonate hardness in an acidified aquarium water will be almost always under 1°GH, despite what the pH is.

On the other hand, there is a strong mutual relationship between pH and carbonate hardness in alkaline water because there is much carbonate and bicarbonate salts dissolved in this type of water. If the pH is high, carbonate hardness will also be high. Therefore, by measuring the pH you can guess the carbonate hardness. Keeping this relationship in mind, you can control the quality of water used, this being the secret to breeding discus.

-WHEN CARBONATE HARDNESS IS HIGH

Buffer action is greater in water showing a high carbonate hardness, having a greater potential to neutralize nitric acid. When tap water showing more than 5°GH is set out through aeration, the pH will be above 8. The dry season breeding method can be used for this type of water. The reason for this is because if the rainy season method is used, the aquarium water pH will always be alkaline. Breeding discus at that pH level is not possible and their beautiful colors will not be at their best. Also, reproduction is practically impossible.

If using the dry season method, it will take many days for the pH to become acid. But, once the pH decreases it can be brought to the ideal level by water changes. Even if the original pH level is high, reproduction can be possible by controlling the amount of water changed, holding its pH at about 6.0-6.9. To know how much water to change, you have to keep data on how much was changed every time this is done. For instance, if 25% of the water was changed when its pH was 5.0 and it went up to 7.2 after the water change, then change only 20% of the water next time. By repeating this process, calculate how much water was changed from the time the pH was 5.0 until it reaches 6.9.

-WHEN CARBONATE HARDNESS IS TOO HIGH

If the pH of the water is over 10.0 even after aeration, this water is considered to have a high hardness. When this happens, this water can easily be softened by boiling it. This changes the bicarbonate salt, leaving only carbonate to settle in the water.

This is a very hard task, so be prepared to do the hard work of handling large amounts of water. It will be a lot easier if an ion exchange resin is available.

-WHEN CARBONATE HARDNESS IS TOO LOW

Water low in carbonate hardness is more suitable for use in the rainy season breeding method but it can also be used for the dry season method. Also, such water can be used in a method fitting in between those two. It's a method of changing the water every day or once every 2-3 days.

When carbonate hardness is too low in the water used for the dry season method, the pH will decrease rapidly. Therefore, you will have to change the water more frequently. This will obviously differ depending upon the amount and size of the fish, size of the aquarium, and the amount of food given. When you have two parents (a pair) in a 150 liter aquarium, you have to change about 50% of the water once a week.

-WHEN THE CARBONATE HARDNESS CHANGES

Be careful of the daily change in water quality when using tap water. Tap water that originates from the shallow underground waters of a mountainside will change depending upon the weather. If such a location is in a cold climate, this water may change only in the wintertime or at springtime when the snow starts to melt. When this happens, an abnormal change will take place not only in carbonate hardness, but also in other substances as well. Depending upon the location, the water quality will change within one to two days after the rain.

When using this type of water, it is safer to use an intermediate-rainy season breeding method, keeping the change in water quality to a minimum by reducing the amount of water changed at

one time. Either way you choose, keep data on the changes of water quality and choose a day when the water quality is stable to change it.

-PREPARING THE NEW WATER

When the amount to be changed is small, tap water is safe to use as long as its temperature is adjusted. However, when you are changing large amounts of water, sterilizers in the water (chlorine) must be neutralized by the use of a counteragent. Because carbon dioxide cannot be removed as fast, aerate the water in a different aquarium for half to a full day beforehand.

UNTESTABLE WATER QUALITY

What decides whether reproduction will occur is a suitable water quality, a well mated pair, your breeding technique, and spawning conditions. The most important factor among all these is the water quality.

-WATER QUALITY SUITABLE FOR REPRODUCTION

As I studied the relationship between reproduction and water quality through actual experience, I came to think that water quality cannot be determined only by what is indicated in numbers.

I experienced cases in which, even though the pH and water hardness were the same, reproduction was successful in some aquaria but in others it was a failure. This means that other factors besides the pH and hardness are affecting reproduction.

Based on this, I have decided to call this kind of quality that cannot be shown in numbers "untestable water quality," and the quality that is generally used (water quality shown in numbers with pH, hardness, or NO2 concentration) "testable quality."

After many different experiences, I came to the conclusion that reproduction in fishes cannot take place only with the testable water quality. Nor can reproduction take place only by fitting the testable water quality within the breeding water quality range. In short, besides the testable water quality, the untestable water quality also has to fit within the breeding water quality range. From this we can see that there is a wide range between the testable and untestable water quality suitable for reproduction of easily reproducing fish, but, on the other hand, a narrow range between these water qualities suitable for the reproduction of not so easily reproducing fish.

-WHAT IS UNTESTABLE WATER QUALITY

What determines the untestable water quality? Not only in the case of the discus, reproduction occurs when the fish's health condition (absorption of nutrition and hormone balance) is at its best. This is greatly related to the ecosystem created by the microorganisms found in the filter, digestive bacteria inside the fish's digestive organs, and to the testable water quality of the aquarium water.

The filter bacteria have the function of changing ammonia to nitrous acid and nitrous acid to nitric acid, contributing greatly to the testable water quality. However, it is thought that it is somehow affecting the fish's health in a more direct way. Untestable water quality defines this delicate quality of the water produced by the ecosystem of microorganisms.

Therefore, untestable water quality is determined by the kinds of filter and digestive bacteria, their association, and percentage.

There are many different kinds of filter and digestive bacteria. Considering the possibilities of their association and percentage, the ecosystem formed as a whole will probably be a very complex one. From this, we can see that controlling the untestable water quality as we do the testable water quality will be very difficult. Even if it is controlled, when the ecosystem of one microorganism changes to another's ecosystem, it will require a certain period of time until it stabilizes. If the untestable water quality is not suitable for the discus to reproduce, then this will not occur. I think that the reason why the reproduction of discus is so difficult is because it is difficult to control the untestable water quality.

-HOW TO DISTINGUISH THE GOOD FROM THE BAD UNTESTABLE WATER QUALITY

An aquarist with the goal of reproducing his fish has to choose the most suitable untestable water quality for that purpose. How is this done? As discussed earlier, since the ecosystem of microorganisms is impossible to determine, it becomes fundamental to check the fish's health condition.

The checkpoints are many, from the way they eat to body color and swimming behavior, but the easiest way is to check the color of their eyes. From my experience, their health condition is at its best when they show red color around their eyes, except when the redness is temporary due to the use of hormones. Most will have redness showing while they are exhibiting reproductive behavior or prior to it. Apparently, even a young fish will have the redness if the untestable water quality is suitable.

However, reproduction will not necessarily be an immediate success if the fish was kept in a different aquarium before, and then put into a new, more suitable one. As will be discussed later, this is due to what I call "adaptation," which has not been allowed to occur.

-WHY DOES UNTESTABLE WATER CHANGE?

In discus breeding, there are many cases in which, although reproduction was successful once, it will not continue. The reason for this could be that there was a change in the untestable water quality. This may mean that a great variation occurred in the ecosystem of microorganisms, causing it to change. This variation may have been caused by many reasons, but there are two very important ones. The first is a large amount of water changed and a thorough filter cleaning.

The testable water quality is greatly changed when a large amount of water is changed. The microorganisms' influential percentage and association will be greatly affected by this. Most of the microorganisms, such as filter bacteria, will be washed away by a thorough cleaning of the filter. However, those that take over in the aquarium next are not necessarily the same microorganisms as before.

Another reason is the excessive use of medicines. It is not hard to imagine what the use of large doses of antibiotics or sulfa drugs can do to an ecosystem of microorganisms. Therefore, if you must use such drugs, use the right kind and according to prescription. The use of medicine without knowing its effectiveness to the disease may destroy any chances of reproduction.

Also, the discus's vital resistance power will be radically reduced by the use of medicine, making them susceptible to other diseases as well. Be especially careful when using antibiotics.

Even the use of formalin can cause damage to microorganisms. However, depending on its dosage, it will not affect the untestable water quality and may even stimulate the fish to reproduce. Medicine can be a plus or a minus, depending on how it is used.

-HOW DOES TESTABLE WATER QUALITY AFFECT THE UNTESTABLE?

We have been discussing the testable water quality changes during the course of breeding. Wouldn't this kind of change affect the ecosystem of microorganisms?

I conducted an experiment on this matter using pH, the easiest of testable water quality, as an indicator. The method is as follows: When the pH of the aquarium in which the discus are continuously reproducing reaches 4.5, bring it back to 6.8 by adding sodium bicarbonate. Repeat the process once the pH is 4.5 again. After repeating this process about five times, bring the pH back to 6.8 by changing the water this time (to remove sodium nitrate). Of course, pH 4.5-6.8 is the discus's breeding water quality range.

The result in my tanks was that the discus continued to reproduce. This means that this range of fluctuation of pH does not affect the stabilized ecosystem of microorganisms, therefore not causing any change in the untestable water quality.

WHY ISN'T REPRODUCTION SUCCESSFUL?

We have discussed reproduction with regard to its being hindered by a change in the untestable water quality. Now let's discuss all the reasons for an unsuccessful reproduction.

-WHEN EGGS DO NOT HATCH

On many occasions the male discus is too young and unable to fertilize the eggs. If this is the case, you may continue the breeding while maintaining the same unstable water quality.

-WHEN TWO FISH ARE WELL PAIRED BUT UNABLE TO CONTINUE SPAWNING

In such cases, consider the testable and untestable water qualities, adaptation, and other reasons.

• A VARIATION IN TESTABLE WATER QUALITY

It is possible the fish is not healthy due to nitrous acid, ammonia, large amounts of iron, or large amounts of nitrate in the water. Also, make sure that the pH is not above 7.0. If this is the case, use proper measuring equipment to keep checking the pH while the water is being changed and adjustments are made.

• A VARIATION IN UNTESTABLE WATER QUALITY

It is possible that the ecosystem of microorganisms is poor and the fish cannot maintain the best health condition. Also, it is possible that one particular microorganism is multiplying at an abnormal rate. I will discuss the measures later.

- ADAPTATION HAS NOT TAKEN PLACE

Both testable and untestable water qualities are within the breeding water quality range but the discus has not yet adapted. I will discuss the details later.

- THE FISH MAY HAVE CONTRACTED A DISEASE

If separating diseases into internal and external diseases, indigestion is especially prominent of the internal diseases, and the causes of external diseases are parasites.

Fish suffering from indigestion can be easily spotted because their excrement is jelly-like. Immediately raise the water temperature to 34°-35°C. By doing this, you'll increase the fish's metabolism and the disease could be cured in about one week. Early discovery is crucial.

There are many kinds of parasites, but in the case of discus, the most common problem is caused by parasites that invade the gills. If this happens, the fish will sometimes have one of the gill covers closed, breathing will be abnormally fast, or the gill cover will overhang. This is called gill disease and is caused by a gill fluke or a close relative of the parasite.

Use formalin or Masoten for treatment. However, since these drugs will destroy the ecosystem of microorganisms, be very careful with the dosage.

- WATER TEMPERATURE MAY BE TOO HIGH

When breeding young fish, water temperatures are set high in many cases because this speeds up the fish's metabolism, thus speeding up the growing process. A suitable average temperature for breeding is around 30°C. It can be set a little lower for the Turquoise and a little higher for the Red Royal Blue or Brown. If it is above 33°C, the success rate for reproduction will suddenly drop.

- NOT ENOUGH OXYGEN IN THE WATER

When there isn't enough oxygen dissolved in the water, the fish will be gasping for air near the surface of the water in a "nose up" position. The situation may not be bad enough for a "nose up," but the fish will still assume such a position when the oxygen consumption increases while it is eating. Supply more oxygen by aeration as a countermeasure.

- NO STIMULATION

When the fish do not spawn even when conditions are favorable, one method is to stimulate them in some way. In an aquarium lacking in stimulation, in many cases the discus's eyes are not colored red.

In such a case, try changing 20% of the water every one or two

189

days. However, be careful not to cause a change in the pH, keeping the water suitable for spawning. This process may cause a slight change in the untestable water quality and the eggs may not be fertilized, but after a while, if the male discus adapts, fertilization will occur.

WHY DO PROFESSIONALS SUCCEED IN REPRODUCTION?

Although a professional breeder will have many mated pairs, those actually used for reproductive purposes are only a few. This means keeping the same few pairs to continue reproducing, and getting many young fish. A good pair can have more than 600 young fish in the period of a month. Having 2-3 pairs continuously reproducing, the number of young fish can be great.

The difference between a professional and an amateur breeder lies in whether he can or cannot maintain continuous reproduction. The amateur will often not be able to do this. This is because he will completely ignore the untestable water quality. Whether the professional is or isn't aware of the untestable water quality, he is still maintaining it.

Whether the breeder is a professional or an amateur, the first successful reproduction could have been purely by coincidence. Only the professional breeder will skillfully maintain the breeding water quality, having the same

pairs reproducing continuously in the same aquarium. Also, he is able to set up another aquarium with the same untestable water quality.

Differences such as these are the same as saying that there is a difference in how the water is sensed or judged by the breeders. While the professional sees that the water in which reproduction was successful is the most suitable, even if it is dirty, the amateur may think only that the most suitable water is clear, clean water.

-SETTING UP AN AQUARIUM WITH THE SAME WATER QUALITY AS THE AQUARIUM IN WHICH REPRODUCTION WAS SUCCESSFUL

In discus breeding, setting up another aquarium with the same water quality as the aquarium in which reproduction was successful is the key to ensure the next reproduction. To set up such aquariums, the following 3 methods are possible:

• USE THE SAME WATER AND FILTER BACTERIA.

Even in an aquarium where the breeding water quality is set up, it is necessary to have the water changed in order to maintain its quality. Instead of throwing away the old water, save it, and by the time you have done a few more water changes, you should have enough to set up another aquarium of the same capacity. When doing this, maintain aeration and proper temperature even if there's only a small amount of water. When you have the amount of water desired, start the filter using a portion of the filter material that was used in the original aquarium. Adjust the testable water quality after one day. This method is the easiest and most accurate of the three.

- USE THE PAIR REPRODUCING SUCCESSFULLY

This method is to put the successful pair in an aquarium where the ecosystem of microorganisms has not yet formed. Bacteria suitable for reproduction exist in the pair's digestive organs. Because there should be a close relationship between the digestive bacteria and the filter bacteria, it is expected that the digestive bacteria that are expelled from the fish's body through its excrement find the proper filter bacteria and increase it. Of course, the testable water quality should be within the breeding water quality range before the pair is added to the aquarium.

Since this method has a somewhat poor percentage rate, it should be for the more experienced breeder.

- REPEAT THE SAME BREEDING METHOD USED IN THE FEW MONTHS BEFORE REPRODUCTION OCCURRED

Once reproduction has taken place, try to remember how you kept the aquarium. You have to remember at least three months back or, in some cases, six months. Try to remember how often and how much of the water was changed, what kinds and how much food were given, the kinds of neutralizers used, and any other keeping methods, and repeat the process. Naturally, also use the same utensils and fixtures.

The disadvantage of this method is that it is time-consuming and the success rate is not very good. However, if your goal is continuous reproduction, remembering and organizing such procedures can be useful in future spawnings. Also, it teaches you the importance of keeping data or notes about such things as aquarium maintenance.

-IT TAKES TIME TO ADAPT

In discus breeding it is necessary that the testable and untestable water qualities are both within the breeding water quality range. However, reproduction will not take place only because such criteria are met. The fish put into the aquarium will gradually change its body to reproduce in the new kind of water. The way in which the fish's body gets used to the new breeding water quality is what I call "adaptation."

Even when keeping the fish in a proper breeding water quality, there are cases in which the female will spawn but the male will not fertilize the eggs. This generally means that the female has adapted faster than the male, or that the female has a wider range of untestable water quality than the male.

Therefore, a certain period of waiting must be allowed until the male adapts to the untestable water quality. From my experiences, it will take a male from half a year to a full year to adapt. This is why it is important to keep the fish in the breeding quality water from its younger stages. By doing this the percentage of fertilized eggs from the first spawning after the fish matures will be high.

-FLUCTUATION AND ADAPTATION OF UNTESTABLE WATER QUALITY

Let us say, for instance, that there is a breeding place (A) and a breeding place (B), and that each has a pair that are continually spawning. What would happen if the pairs were exchanged?

These pairs had continued spawning in the testable and untestable water qualities of their original breeding places.

However, even if the testable water quality of each breeding place was the same, this doesn't mean the same applies for the untestable water quality. Therefore, both pairs will stop reproducing until they can adapt to their new breeding place's (6 months to a year) untestable water quality. Therefore, even if you purchase a well-mated pair from a shop, it will take at least six months to a year before they will satisfactorily reproduce.

There are some exceptions. Sometimes spawning will take place within a half to a full month after they have been moved to a new place. It's the same with newly purchased pairs or newly purchased fish that have paired and spawned right away.

Essentially, reproduction should not have taken place when there was a change in the testable water quality. But, because this quality is a product of the ecosystem of microorganisms, it takes a while for the change to appear in the fish's body. In other words, even if the untestable water quality

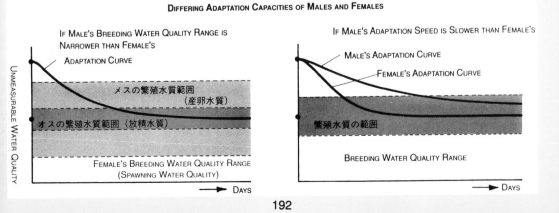

DIFFERING ADAPTATION CAPACITIES OF MALES AND FEMALES

IF MALE'S BREEDING WATER QUALITY RANGE IS NARROWER THAN FEMALE'S

ADAPTATION CURVE

メスの繁殖水質範囲
（産卵水質）

オスの繁殖水質範囲（放精水質）

FEMALE'S BREEDING WATER QUALITY RANGE
(SPAWNING WATER QUALITY)

UNMEASURABLE WATER QUALITY

→ DAYS

IF MALE'S ADAPTATION SPEED IS SLOWER THAN FEMALE'S

MALE'S ADAPTATION CURVE

FEMALE'S ADAPTATION CURVE

繁殖水質の範囲

BREEDING WATER QUALITY RANGE

→ DAYS

changes, it will take a while to affect the fish. Therefore, the fish will have its previous constitution and reproduction can occur.

Therefore, when the effect of the change in unstable water quality begins to appear after a half to a full month, the hatching percentage will drop and reproduction will fail to take place. Soon, the eggs will not even be fertilized and, in some cases, not even spawned. However, if the untestable water quality of the new breeding place is within the range of breeding water quality, the fish will spawn once again in six months to a year, when adaptation is completed. In this case, because the female will adapt

by another male, it will never be allowed enough time to adapt and produce fertilized eggs. Patiently wait and keep them in the same untestable water quality for spawning to take place.

When the male's body starts to adapt to the new breeding water quality, some eggs may be fertilized, although this is only in a few cases. As spawning continues, so will the number of fertilized eggs increase. Soon more than 95% will be fertilized.

Looking at it this way, the relationship of the testable and untestable water qualities is represented as in the figure. The vertical line represents the testable water quality, the horizontal line represents the untestable water quality and their changes. Points A through E are all within the breeding water quality range, therefore reproduction is possible. If a pair is reproducing at the A water quality, it will continue to reproduce even if moved to B or C. Also, the same can be said of a pair reproducing at D water quality when moved to E. The reason for this is that as long as the change in testable water quality is within the breeding water quality range, reproduction is not affected.

However, when a pair reproducing at A water quality is moved to D, or if a pair reproducing at E water quality is moved to B, reproduction will stop. Even if there was no change in the testable water quality, there was a change in the untestable.

RELATIONSHIP BETWEEN TESTABLE AND UNTESTABLE WATER QUALITY

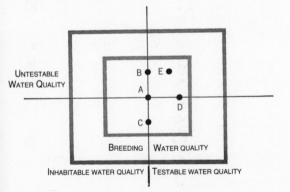

faster, spawning will occur but until the male adapts, fertilization will not. The reason that there are so many cases of unfertilized eggs in discus breeding is because it takes time for the male to adapt. If the male itself is blamed for unfertilized eggs and is replaced

Considering this fact by using the same pair, the greater the change in the untestable water quality, the longer it takes for adaptation. In other words, when the same pair is moved from A to D, it will take longer to reproduce than when the pair is moved from A to B.

Naturally, there will be individual differences in the speed of adaptation. In general, males adapt slower than females, but there will still be a difference among the males themselves. . Therefore, a good pair is a pair that adapts quickly, especially when the male does so. In other words, the important factor in reproduction is whether the male is a good one or a bad one. A professional breeder can select good pairs from the many he has and succeeds in continuous spawnings.

A good pair will not stop reproducing with only a slight change in the untestable water quality. And, once completely adapted, the spawning amount is large and the hatching rate is high, producing healthy young fish. Pairs such as this can have 200-300 young in one spawning.

FACTS ON SPAWNING
Raising Techniques

-YOUNG OR MATURE FISH, WHICH ONES TO BUY

When spawning is the goal, we are always unsure of which fish size to get. Especially if the breeder is going to try spawning them for the first time, he will not be sure whether to get young fish, adults, or a pair. The difference is not that great if money is not a problem. This is because, if the fish are young, it will take them about one year until they reach maturity and have continuous spawning. But even if the fish is mature, it'll also take about one year until they adapt to the untestable water quality.

However, keep in mind the advantages and disadvantages each has. You can judge the body and color of an adult fish or a pair, but in the case of a young fish, judgment is difficult unless you are a very experienced breeder. The advantage of choosing young fish is that you can raise them to be suitable for reproduction. While removing those prone to contracting diseases, having bad temperament, and those sensitive to even a slight change in water quality, the chances of forming good pairs are better.

-HOW TO SET UP A DIFFERENT AQUARIUM WITH THE SAME UNTESTABLE WATER QUALITY.

To efficiently raise young fish until they reproduce, consistently keep them in the same untestable water quality. However, actually, this is not very easy. Sometimes you may have to use medications if the fish contract a disease or have parasites and, sometimes the

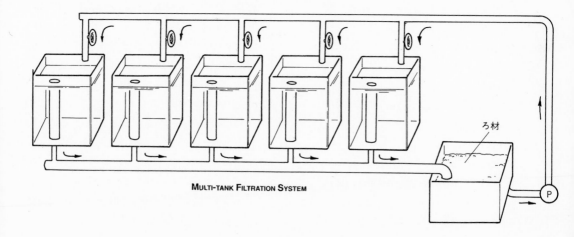

ろ材

P

fish may have to be moved due to unexpected problems. Also, if the breeding has progressed normally and a pair was formed, you may have to remove the remaining fish to a different aquarium, leaving only the pair so that the untestable water quality is not changed. However, if you want to form another pair from the remaining fish, they also must be kept in the same untestable water quality.

If the goal is reproduction, you must set up a few more aquaria with the same untestable water quality. By doing so, you save time consumed in adaptation and can continue with their reproduction.

As previously discussed, there are three different methods of setting up such aquariums. However, I would like to introduce two methods that are more purposeful and systematic.

-CONCENTRATED FILTER SYSTEM

In this method, only one filter is used in a few or many aquariums. This setup has the filtered water returned to each aquarium and gets back to the filter through an overflow system.

This method can be very convenient depending upon how it is used. It allows you to to use the aquariums you need, leaving the unused aquariums to keep extra water to be used as a replacement.

However, there are a few things to be cautious about, especially when it comes to diseases. Since the same water is dispensed to all aquaria, there is the danger of a disease spreading to all of them. It is the same in the case of parasites.

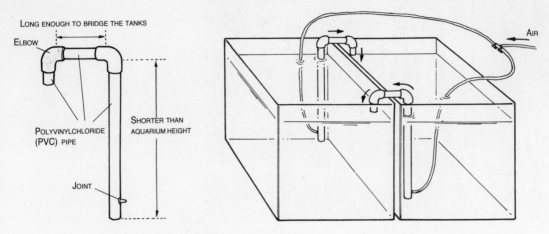

LONG ENOUGH TO BRIDGE THE TANKS

ELBOW

AIR

POLYVINYLCHLORIDE
(PVC) PIPE

SHORTER THAN
AQUARIUM HEIGHT

JOINT

LONG ENOUGH TO EXTEND A LITTLE ABOVE WATER LEVEL

-DOUBLE AIR-LIFT METHOD

Since the concentrated filter system is so elaborate, it is more for the professional breeder. Compared to this, when you want to add only one or two more aquaria, this next method is more convenient.

Put the new aquarium beside the aquarium used now. Try to use the same size aquarium and the same filter system. It is especially important to use the same filter and filter material. This is obvious because you want to create an ecosystem of microorganisms that have the same purpose.

After the new aquarium is set up, add the water, adjust the temperature, and start the filter. At this point the ecosystem of the microorganisms has not yet been formed in the new aquarium. Next, set up the two aquariums with U-shaped pipes as shown in the figure and set up an air-lift through them. Through this air-lift

water from the new aquarium will flow to the original and vice-versa.

When doing this, keep the amount of air set on low, allowing only a little water to go through. The standard amount of water flow is to have half of the water in the original aquarium exchanged in two to three days. After this you can either keep the air-lift going or stop it after two to three weeks.

Having two or three aquariums set up using this method can be very convenient. For instance, if you have two 60 cm aquariums set up, one can be used for breeding while the other can be used to keep replacement water. Compared to when breeding with only one aquarium, the change in water quality is small since there is twice as much water and, besides, it saves tampering with the breeding aquarium.

Also, if one aquarium is drained, the breeding aquarium will continue to operate and, once

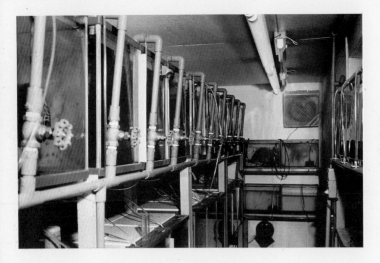

A typical set-up with multiple tanks and a plumbing system that allows adjustment of the water flow to each tank.

water is replaced in the drained aquarium, the air-lift can be restarted and water will be slowly exchanged. When changes in water quality are this gentle, it gives you an advantage when trying to have the fish spawn.

-CHOOSE FISH IN GOOD HEALTH

When setting up a new aquarium, the ecosystem of microorganisms has not yet formed. Whether you can create an ecosystem of beneficial microorganisms or not is what controls the breeding difficulty level later on.

Usually, to create an ecosystem of microorganisms that are beneficial, use the method of transferring the water or filter material used in an aquarium that already has the desired ecosystem. However, this method cannot be used by those who have never kept an aquarium.

If this is the case, it is important to choose fish in good health. An ecosystem of beneficial microorganisms already exists in the digestive organs of such fish and these can be used to create the same in an aquarium.

If an unhealthy fish, for example one with indigestion or poor coloration and appetite, is put into the aquarium, an ecosystem of harmful microorganisms may be created making breeding very difficult. First-time breeders must check the fish's health condition very carefully before purchasing them.

TO HAVE GOOD PAIRS

As discussed in the beginning, there are different methods of breeding discus. The most suitable method should be chosen by taking into consideration the quality of the tap water being used, location in which the aquarium is set up, and how much time the breeder can spend caring for the aquarium.

The important thing to remember when purchasing

young fish for spawning purposes is to choose healthy fish of the same size.

The number of fish to purchase depends on the size aquariums you have, but it is best to buy a little more than enough. If the number of fish is small, they will tend to be shy and hide away in a corner and not eat well, thus not growing much.

Even in cases when they grow at a normal rate, the young fish will fight each other, resulting in the weaker not growing or, in some cases, perishing. Purchasing larger quantities is a preventive measure to such problems.

There are many different kinds of live, frozen, and dried foods, but try to combine two or three different kinds and feed mainly that which the fish seem to favor the most. As they grow, their taste in food may change. In such cases, feed them what they favor the most at that point. This is because the required nutrition differs according to their developmental stage and aquarium conditions.

-SELECTION OF FISH IN THEIR EARLY STAGES

• **Deformed fish**.- It's important to sort out the individuals not suitable for reproduction while in their early stage. It's especially important to sort out those with deformities in their reproductive organs. There are cases in which even if a pair formed and spawning took place, the eggs would not attach to the spawning substrate, or the eggs were not fertilized even though an attempt at fertilization did take place. These fish cannot be cured, nor can this be covered up with techniques.

• **Fish with abnormal personality**. There will always be a dominant fish among the many being kept. However, you must sort out those abnormally dominant. In most cases, these will not remain as a pair even if they become parents.

• **Fish susceptible to diseases**.- Some will be more susceptible to diseases than others. A fish that keeps contracting the same disease is, of course, not suitable for pairing in the future. However, do not conclude that the fish was born weak because it may just be weakened from not being able to adapt to the aquarium's water quality. In some cases the fish's health will return once the water quality changes for the better. Experience is needed to distinguish one from another. Fish susceptible to parasites are also not suitable.

• **Fish with especially poor growth**.- Fish with poor appetite and extremely poor growth are also not suitable for purposes of reproduction. Sort out such fish and keep them in a different aquarium.

-TO HAVE GOOD PAIRS FROM PARENT FISH

Have a few parent fish in a 90 cm tank. Purchased fish or ones acquired from friends will need some time until they can be paired because of the change in the untestable water quality. Those gathered from their natural habitat will especially need more time than those cultured.

When the acquired fish had already been kept in a regularized untestable water quality and in the testable water quality fitting the breeding water quality range, pairs will begin to form within a half to a full month.

If this is the case, maintain the pH between 5.5-6.9 and continue to breed them in a regularized untestable water quality. Pairs should begin to form as the fish begin to adapt to the untestable water quality.

-MEASURES TO TAKE WHEN PAIRS DO NOT FORM

Sometimes no pairs will form even though the fish were kept within the breeding water quality for a long time. The common cause in cases such as this is the fish's poor health condition.

Except in special types, the condition of a discus's health can be determined by the color of their eyes. If the redness around their eyes is light, or if there is no redness at all, it's impossible to form pairs.

Also, make sure the water temperature is not too high. This varies with the fish, but they should usually be kept between 28° and 32°C.

In general, the health condition of fish kept with the rainy season breeding method is good and they have a nice red coloration around the eyes. However, the pH tends to be higher than the breeding water quality and because of this there are cases in which pairs do not form.

As a common method, change the breeding method to the intermediate rainy season breeding method and decrease the amount of water changed. However, some fish will show irregularity with a sudden change in the breeding method, so do it gradually.

Fish kept in the dry season breeding method will in many cases not show redness around their eyes and will not form pairs even after one or two years. Cases such as this are especially seen in the Turquoise discus. As a treatment measure, change only a small amount of water (about 20%) every day.

Sometimes pairs will not form due to an unbalanced diet. In such a case, add a multivitamin in liquid or powdered form to the food. Keep the dosage small, never giving too much. Carefully read and follow label instructions.

It is very difficult to determine whether the problem is a lack of vitamins. Because of this, try adding some plants to the aquarium and use this as an indicator. Choose plants with relatively soft leaves such as *Ambulia* or water sprite. Fish lacking in vitamins will eat such leaves. As the vitamin is supplied, the amount of leaves eaten should decrease.

-MEASURES TO TAKE ONCE A PAIR HAS FORMED

Once a pair has formed, either the remaining fish or the new pair should be moved to a different aquarium. As a fundamental rule, considering the relation with the untestable water quality, it's best to leave the pair and move the other fish. When doing this, it is convenient to have another aquarium set up with the same untestable water quality beforehand.

Once the pair is alone, they will usually proceed on to the spawning behavior, but, at times, some will begin to fight. Except for those that will stop fighting in 2-3 days, those that continue to fight should be stopped somehow. The most common method would be to add one or two more discus to the aquarium. By doing so, the pair arranged will be reformed. If they tend to be territorial, the new pair can be separated from the others by putting a divider in the aquarium after 2-3 days. By keeping the other fish in the pair's view, they should stop fighting.

However, sometimes even this will not stop the pair from fighting. If this is the case, they

should be returned to the original group and the pairing tried again.

-SETTING UP OF THE SPAWNING SUBSTRATE

Discus will display the pairing behavior by facing each other and spreading their dorsal and caudal fins while keeping their heads tilted slightly downward. When spawning approaches they will begin to shake the front half of their bodies.

Before the fish spawn, set up a spawning area using such things sold in the market as spawning tubes, PVC pipes, bricks, or driftwood. The spawning angle is usually from 60° to 90° but will sometimes be horizontal. If the spawning substrate is not to the fish's liking, they may spawn on whatever is available, even the surface of the filter. Since the angle of spawning is not a problem, the type of spawning substrate and its location should be determined while considering the pair's spawning habit.

The location for spawning varies according to each pair, but one common factor remains, they always choose a place where the current is slow. The reason for this is thought to be that by doing so, they are increasing the chances for fertilization to take place since the amount of the male's sperm is very small. Therefore, try to place the spawning substrate away from a fast current.

Once a pair has found an

acceptable spawning location they will begin cleaning it with their mouths. At about this time a long, thick (compared with that of the male) ovipositor emerges from the female's body. This is how we distinguish which is the male and which is the female.

The time from when the cleaning begins until the actual spawning takes place is from 2-3 hours to half a day, a little short compared to other American cichlids.

SPAWNING SEQUENCE
SPAWNING BEHAVIOR

As the cleaning stage nears its end, the female will touch her spawning tube to the lower part of the spawning substrate and start to move slowly upward. Then, the male will participate and spawning begins. Depending upon the pair, the male may participate after the actual egg deposition has begun.

The eggs will be laid in neat straight rows and the male will follow closely, fertilizing them. This process is repeated for about 30 minutes to an hour and the number of eggs will be about 200 to 300.

However, not all pairs will behave like this. The male may at times be a bystander while the female is laying the eggs. Some males may eat the eggs while they are being laid. These males are either too young or still not adapted to the untestable water quality.

Such males may partially show spawning behavior, such as cleaning, but will not fertilize or show the instinctive behavior of protecting the eggs. However, even males such as these will eventually begin to protect the eggs once adaptation is completed. Fish with the unusual habit of eating their eggs are very rare.

HATCHING

Once spawning is complete the pair, together and sometimes taking turns, will start a continuous current by using their pectoral fins or mouth. If the water temperature is around 30°C, hatching will take place in about 50 hours. Once hatched, the babies will be connected to the spawning substrate at their head area by a bonding string. A healthy baby will constantly wiggle its tail.

If the parents are not very happy with the location, they may move the babies to a better location by using their mouths. The babies will grow by feeding on the yolk sac located in their abdominal area. The yolk sac will no longer be present after about two days. Their bodies will become thinner and longer compared to the time of hatching.

At this stage the babies will begin to move more actively, wrapping themselves around the bonding string in groups ranging from a few to as many as 10-20.

In cases where the young are weak, this type of activity does not take place. Also, because of the weakness of the bonding string, the babies will break away from the spawning substrate. Because of this, the parent fish will try to collect the fallen fish and put them back in their original spot. However, in most cases they will fall again. After two days these babies will be gone.

Sometimes, babies will not be able to absorb their nourishment, causing the yolk sac to expand. The reason for the expansion of the yolk sac is that it absorbs water. When this happens, due to the weight of the yolk sac the babies will flip on their back and also disappear after 3-4 days.

The cause of such weak babies lies in the parents. This can happen especially when the parents are not adapted to the water quality or when there is a great difference in the suitability of the untestable water quality between the male and the female.

The first problem stated can be solved over time, but to solve the latter the pair must be rearranged. Sometimes, the reason for weak babies is due to the fact that the parents come from poor bloodlines. In this case, the pair also needs to be rearranged.

SWIMMING

About 2-3 days after hatching, the bonding strings will break and the young will begin to swim. The parents, to counter this, will take the babies in their mouths and attempt to put them back in place. This is the busiest time in the spawning cycle. It is thought that this behavior helps the babies become aware of their parents.

Soon, the babies will begin to swim close to the parents' bodies. This is referred to as "contacting." The babies will begin to eat a secreted substance from the parents which is referred to as "milk," and will grow at a surprisingly fast rate.

Normally, after 5 days of this nursing process, the babies will still not feed on newly hatched brine shrimp. After about 6 days, however, they will start to prey upon the brine shrimp, but the number of days until this begins to happen will vary.

SEPARATING THE YOUNG FISH

Once the babies begin to feed on the brine shrimp they can be separated from their parents. If the number of fish is small (50 or fewer) they can remain with their parents for about a month. But if the number of fish exceeds 200, the parents will be exhausted and you must continue to feed these babies brine shrimp. If you neglect to do this, you might interfere with the next spawning cycle. When the number of babies is large, and you are sure they have begun to feed on the brine shrimp, you may separate them from their parents. When putting them into another aquarium, be sure that the water quality is the same. Pay special attention to the untestable water quality.

RAISING THE YOUNG

A 45 cm or 60 cm aquarium is best for raising the young. Do not place any sand on the bottom and aerate the aquarium using an air stone set on low. Use a sponge-type filter in the tank. This is to prevent wasting brine shrimp by them being sucked into the filter or their remains from decreasing the quality of the water.

Since brine shrimp can survive in fresh water for a few hours, portion the food out so that the babies can eat them all within that period of time. Brine shrimp is easily digested and absorbed, not causing a decrease in the pH. Therefore, it is considered an excellent food.

After 1-2 weeks, try to give the young fish small amounts of finely chopped beefheart, making the replacement while checking how well they are eating it. Once the fry begin to feed on the beefheart the decrease in the pH will be faster. Therefore, the water will have to be changed more frequently. Change 20% to 25% of the water once every 1-3 days, making sure leftover food is removed. Gradually raise the water temperature and maintain it fairly high (32-33°C).

By the time the babies are over 2 cm in diameter, they will be a little stronger and able to endure a change in the untestable water quality. You will be able to move them into a different aquarium and also be able to choose from the rainy, intermediate, or dry season breeding methods. If you choose the dry season breeding method, remember to use a relatively powerful filter.

TYPE OF FILTER TO USE IN SPAWNING AQUARIUM

Reproduction is possible no matter what kind of filter is used. It doesn't even have to be an especially powerful one. However, filters that will suck in a newly hatched fish must be avoided or at least its structure should be modified.

I use a handmade sponge filter. There are many advantages to using this kind of filter, such as: it will not suck in the baby fish, its coverage area is wide, its effective period is long, it allows the speculation of untestable water quality to be made by how dirty the filter material is, it is easy to change the filter material, the amount of filtered water can be controlled by the amount of air flow, and there is a good chance that the eggs will be spawned on the PVC pipe used.

The point to remember when spawning discus is to breed them in a regularized untestable water quality. In other words, in water that has an ecosystem of the same microorganisms over a long period of time.

A Southeast Asian discus with excellent body shape.

Most discus breeders have double rows of tanks that are easily accessible for feeding and maintenance. Spawning tanks are either on the upper level or secluded in another, less busy, part of the room.

香港ブリーダー
からの
メッセージ

A MESSAGE FROM A HONG KONG BREEDER

Lo Wing Yat, Sunny

It was late in 1980 when I first started breeding discus. My experiences for the previous 20 years were the breeding and reproducing of a variety of marine fishes, and the experiments on ecology during my college years.

Success or failure when breeding aquatic animals, no matter what kind, depends upon the maintenance of water quality, adequate food, and prevention of disease.

Based on this, I began by conducting basic research on the discus's environment and ecology. By doing so, I came to believe that the reason why there are still so many problems existing even today, when the breeding of discus has become so popular, is because the aquarist is not breeding them using the proper methods.

Looking more closely at this proper breeding method theory, it will naturally be linked to the reproduction method. Luckily, I was able to acquire many necessary sources in order to produce a new color variation through some good friends in West Germany, Dr. Eduard Schmidt-Focke, and the United States, Mr. Jack Wattley. By having these fish with which to mate to the Thai discus I was keeping, I was able to produce my own discus line.

Here, I would like to share with you the breeding method of the discus produced from this experiment and the problems encountered while creating the new line.

WATER MAINTENANCE

Originally, the discus lived in stagnant water such as in the tranquil swampy pools or calm streams of the Amazon. In such water, acidity is stable, there aren't many minerals in it, but it is rich with a variety of organic chemicals released by plants. However, when breeding the discus, there is no need to exactly simulate such water conditions. To recreate the balance of nature in an enclosed environment is extremely difficult. After all, the discus is a fish with the ability to adapt.

WATER TEMPERATURE

The discus is a fish that favors high temperatures. Therefore, it is best to keep them in temperatures between 27-32°C. Spawning is possible even at 24-25°C, but avoid this as much as possible because it may lower the fish's metabolism, decreasing its appetite and making it susceptible to diseases.

Raise young fish under 10 months of age at 30°-32°C. This will not only stimulate growth but also prevent problems that can lead to illness. On the other hand, keep mature or parent fish at lower temperatures, between 28° and 30°C, because metabolic stimulation can, in their case, lead to aging.

In fact, there is no need to maintain a stable water temperature in either case. A healthy fish will not contract a disease with a fluctuation of 4° or 5°C. A slight fluctuation in the water temperature during one day may even stimulate spawning.

Diseases can also be treated by raising the water temperature. Discus can be kept at 35°C, and if there is proper aeration they can live for a few hours even at 38.5°C. There aren't too many parasites that can endure such high temperatures. If the fish is aged, weakened, or seriously infected with *Hexamita* disease, raise the water temperature to 35-37°C for three to five days. After doing this, as they are moved to an aquarium set at 33-35°C, their metabolism will accelerate, the stress will be gone, and they will recuperate. Even external injuries caused when handling them will be cured by using this method.

Treatments will be more effective by using this method along with some medicine. For instance, to treat hole-in-the-head disease, the most effective way is to use Metronidazole or other antibiotics and keep water temperatures at 35°C.

pH VALUE

I have successfully kept discus at pH values as low as 4.6 and as high as 8.0, but it is best to keep them at 5.5-6.8. I had almost no problems with external parasites such as fungi or protozoans while I was feeding them at a low pH (5.5). This is because such parasites cannot survive in such acid conditions.

This type of water contains a well balanced ammonia and ammonium content. Ammonia, harmful to all aquatic animals, is released from excrement and bacteria. Ammonia dissolved in water can be decomposed to a harmless ammonium ion as pH decreases. In other words, the higher the pH, the higher the ammonia rate dissolved in the water.

EFFECT OF pH ON THE CONCENTRATION OF AMMONIA IN AN AQUARIUM

pH	AMMONIA %	AMMONIUM ION %
6	0	100
7	1	99
8	4	96
9	25	75
10	78	22

A sudden change in the pH will damage the discus's delicate skin and gills, or even cause it to perish. Remember, an increase in pH has more impact than a decrease.

For example, if you move a fish from an aquarium with a pH in the 5.5-6.8 range into another aquarium with half that pH value, this will not result in fatal problems. However, if the fish is moved into an aquarium with only 0.2 more than the original aquarium's pH, the gills may disintegrate, the fins may become frayed, and a milky substance may form on the skin.

Considering these facts, always test the pH whenever moving the discus, adding more fish to an aquarium, or changing large amounts of water.

There are two ways to decrease the pH. First, I would like to introduce you to how to use the most commonly available natural acid, phosphoric acid. It is sold at local drug stores in a clear liquid form. Concentrated phosphoric acid has corrosive action, so be very careful when handling it and keep it away from children.

To make water more acid, first dilute the concentrated phosphoric acid by a factor of five, siphon about 1 cc into a disposable plastic syringe, and add it to the water in one squeeze. Mix the water until the acid is dissolved and check the pH. If the pH doesn't seem to be getting any lower, continue the injections in small amounts using the same method.

Instead of phosphoric acid, you can also use sodium phosphate (Na_2HPO_4). It comes in a powdered form and can be added directly to the water.

Comparative Chart of Discus Breeders in Japan and Their Methods

DISCUS BREEDERS	SHOP OR BUSINESS	pH	HARDNESS	TO SCREEN OR NOT TO SCREEN THE EGGS	
Okuyama Shoji	Kyoto Okuyama Tropical Fish – Kyoto	5.8 is standard.	I don't care.	I use this method only when the pair has a habit of eating the eggs. It is an effective way to raise the seed parents that you want. I think it is an effective method for selective breeding.	
Nakamura Kazu	Hirosi Pets – Chiba	Start from 6.5 in an aquarium in which the filter is working in order to lower the pH naturally. Egglaying and hatching should occur at about pH 5.5-6.0.	Make KH under 3°.	It is not necessary as long as you keep the quality of the water good.	
Yamada Hiroshi	Guppy Main Shop – Nagano	6.0-6.9 is standard. Egglaying occurs at 4.5 but if it is too low it affects the care later on.	No problems with GH. Make KH as close to 0° as possible.	I have never done it.	
Kurasawa Yasuyuki	Myorenji Aquarium Shop – Kanagawa	5.0-6.3 is standard for turquoise. Brown Discus pose no problem.	Not measured.	I do not use this method.	
Awajiya Kimihiro	Awajiya – Osaka	The pH varies depending upon how the fry were raised. If they were raised in more acid water it should be on the low side; if in less acid water the pH should be closer to neutral (7.0).	Not measured. I wonder if it has any influence?	I think it is good to determine this case by case. I do not do it with my fish.	
Hitsu Shuichi	Discus Institute – Ishikawa	The pH is not monitored. Using only wool in the filter, the pH never goes up. The lower limit is 5.0.	Not measured.	I do not do it. I see no advantages for doing it for the discus.	
Tono Junji	Tono Soft Water Fish Breeders – Osaka	The pH is not monitored. Wait until egglaying and then change one third of the water once every three days.	Not measured.	I do not do it.	
Sawai Seiki	Maraei Ornamental Fish – Osaka	The city water in Kansai is 6.6 to 6.8. Lower it to 5.7.	KH should be 2-3°. The hardness of the city water differs depending upon season and sometimes doesn't work well below 4°.	I use it for the ones that have the bad habit of eating their eggs and fighting. Because of the lack of egg fanning by the parents, a good stream of water is necessary. We can hope that a high percentage of hatching is expected with such a stream.	
Ando Koichi	Discus Peppermint – Gifu	Measuring of pH is not necessary. The standard is 6.7-6.8.	Not measured.	I have no ideas about its good or bad points.	
Harada Tetsuo	Cobalt – Kyoto	The difference in pH depends upon the parents. 5.2-6.7 is the range. There is some hatching at 5.0.	Not measured, but the city water is 3°.	I do it all the time for pairs that are spawning for the first time. Some of the good points are that it teaches the parent fish not to eat the eggs and you can observe the percentage of eggs that are fertilized and hatch. I try not to do it later on.	
Shirase Kozo	Kanagawa	Around 6.0 is standard, but I do not measure exactly.	I use city water of 3°KH, 6°GH.	I don't think it matters either way.	
Yamana Munesa	Aqua Japan – Osaka	Hatching can occur at 5.0, but the upper limit is 6.5.	I use 1°KH, the GH is a little higher.	I do it mostly for first time spawners, especially for the male, mainly to observe the hatching percentage. Sometimes, when the parent fish are not used to spawning, they eat the eggs. I don't use this method very often.	
Nito Katsuhiko	Tokyo	This depends upon the individual fish, but it is around 6.5.	3°-4°GH.	I have never done it.	
Abe Mitsuyoshi	Matsukawaya – Tokyo	It is not measured at present, but before 6.4 was standard.	Not measured.	I never do it. There are some people who take the baby sitting or nursing way.	
Sato Masao	Fish Gallery – Yamanote – Hokkaido	The city water is 7.2 if left for one or two days. The standard is 6.5-6.8.	I do not measure hardness every day because the city water is soft and the hardness low.	There are microbes in the egglaying aquarium and it is effective to cover the eggs so they do not get eaten with the microbes.	
Oshima Masao	R.R.B. Tropical Fish – Saitama	I have no special method for measuring the pH, but the standard is around 6.8, depending upon the water conditions.	I do not measure hardness, but my area it is below 1°KH. I do not care about GH.	I tried it but there were many times where it had no effect.	

HOW TO MAINTAIN WATER QUALITY AFTER THE FRY ARE FREE-SWIMMING	ABOUT ARTIFICIAL HATCHING	ADVICE TO THE READERS
I look after the fry carefully during the period when they are feeding from the parents by watching the pH. After they separate from the parents change 80% of the water.	It will be possible in the future, but I think it is not feasible under the present conditions.	The water conditions are very important, for example checking the pH regularly. It is also important to observe the individual habits of the fish.
I do not feed the parents. They will be okay for up to one month (at most) without food. This way it is easier to care for the water. There are fewer problems when you feed them only a little food.	Changing the water is the point. As the food starts to pollute the water after 3 to 4 hours, it is necessary to change the water completely. It is also important to provide good water quality at all times.	Its rather easy to observe the steps from egglaying to hatching and the change of the water quality and how it affects the fish when they are feeding on the discus milk of the parents or during the two weeks following the time they are separated from the parents. Therefore, you should observe them at all times. It is also necessary to constantly check the pH.
Check the pH. Do not let it get lower than 5.0. When you find it declining, change the proper amount of water to bring it back to the standard value (6.0).	I have tried it but it is very hard work, although one of my favorite kinds of hard work.	You can succeed with pairs in which the eggs do not hatch by maintaining the water quality. It is possible to spend 6 to 12 months to obtain fertilized eggs—so be patient.
A little food may be fed to the parent fish if you wish, but usually I don't feed them until the fry are feeding on baby brine shrimp. I change 25% to 33% of the water after feeding them the brine shrimp.	No experience.	I would like to suggest you try daily care, keeping the seed fish in good healthy conditions.
If the baby fish remain feeding from the parents for three days, apply the proper water change.	No experience.	The types of food and the way it is fed are both equally important. It makes a difference in the quantity and the time of feeding of the discus "hamburger," fresh bloodworms, and frozen bloodworms. Try to combine them all.
Change a maximum of 66% of the water by watching how dirty the water gets.	No experience.	Be patient. That's all.
We continue to feed the parent fish even though the fry are still feeding off them. Change about 70% of the water every day.	The percentage of deformities is so high it is foolish to even try.	Teach the pairs not to eat the eggs. Cover the nest, etc. Try and protect the eggs from fungus by use of medication. When they do get fungus, study the problems one by one until you solve the problems that cause the fungus.
Stop changing water after egglaying. Do nothing until hatching even if the pH goes down. After hatching, change around 20% to 33% of the water and observe the fish.	I don't have enough time. The procedure also requires physical strength so I haven't thought about it.	Keep the pH at the proper level. It is not necessary to think about the water quality more than the condition of the fish. For example, think that the pH of the city water in the Kansai area is 6.0 to 6.5. But it is 7.2 in Yoshino and in Kobe the water is similar to that in Tokyo.
Feed the parents bloodworms if they want to eat while the fry are feeding off the discus milk. Keep an eye on how dirty the water gets. Do not feed them discus "hamburger". Make sure you change the proper amount of water.	It takes too much time. With poor fish growth, I gave up a week after I started.	It is important to raise good strong seed fish.
Raise the temperature of the water to 30°C soon after egglaying. Feed the parents and change enough water to bring the pH back to normal if it has dropped more than 0.5.	I think it is impossible to accomplish because it takes too much time and I do not think it is necessary.	I want you to check the pH because sometimes it depends upon the experience of egglaying on the part of the parent fish. Apply the best way of breeding and adjust it to match each fish and its individual character.
Change 10% to 20% of the water every day after you start to feed the fry baby brine shrimp.	It would be good for business, but I think it takes too much time. I also think that if you have good parent fish you should leave everything to them.	I think there are people who call the discus the "king of tropical fishes." There are many people who use cheap equipment which is not worthy of the value of the discus. If you provide good circumstances for the discus, they will step forward and start breeding.
Do not change water for a week after egglaying. When the fry start feeding from the sides of the parents, gradually change the water by keeping a close eye on the water quality.	I think that raising of the fry by the parents is best. As the percentage of deformities seems high, I am not even considering artificial hatching.	When breeding, putting the emphasis on the variety is what we have to do today. Turquoise discus sold in the market today are from a stable strain. I want you to raise the fish with a good appearance to your eyes using stable specimens of top quality. The fastest way to raise a mated pair will be to raise some of the same size fish that are imported at the same time.
I am trying to keep the pH at 6.0 through water changes. Keep the pH between 5.0 and 6.0.	I have tried it but it takes too much time. It is possible to raise them but it is very hard to look after them by yourself.	As the discus becomes better and easier to get, I think it is a good opportunity for everyone to get the experience. I think it is possible to succeed if you learn to check the pH and how to take care of the water quality.
Reduce the quantity of food for the parents. I seldom use activated carbon.	I hae tried it, but even when the fry appear strong they have many deformities. After all, its better to leave the raising to the parents and natural selection.	I think it is important to keep and raise fish at your own pace.
I change water every day while keeping an eye on its condition.	No experience.	Observe the fish well.
I don't change the water for about two weeks. Feed the fry and the parent fish regularly.	I have tried many times but they grow very slowly. It took half a year to raise three fish by using the yolk of birds eggs.	Because the water quality is different from one place to another, you may get confused listening to others. I am sure you can find the best way to suit your own needs.

Another way is to use peat. This is a collection of moss fibers that are sold in a dried condition. It contains a large amount of tannic acid that is beneficial to fishes living in soft acid waters such as the discus, South American characins, and oviparous medaka.

I use two different kinds of peat moss. The German type has long fibers strung together; the Canadian type is of superior quality, but its structure is brittle and it is in powdered form. A brown liquid can be obtained from the peat by soaking it in hot water for two to three hours. Add one cup at a time to the aquarium until the pH is adjusted to the desired level. You can also use the peat in the filter and adjust the pH by water circulation through it. However, check its quality, for some peat moss will produce the brown liquid but not cause any change in the pH. When you have to increase the pH, you may use sodium bicarbonate, but it is safer to do so by changing the water.

CHANGING WATER

The aquarium water can become polluted through many causes, such as fish excrement, rejected pieces of food, leftover food, and decomposed parts of a dead discus.

The easiest and most direct way to decrease this pollution is to actively change the water. It should be common sense that, if changing more than 30% of the water, the new water's pH should be adjusted to the same level as the aquarium water so as not to shock the discus.

If the new water is slightly alkaline, adjustments can be made easily by diligent water changes. However, change only about 10% of the water at a time because if a large amount of alkaline water is added to the old aquarium water (it has acidified and contains large amounts of ammonium ions) the ammonium ion will change into ammonia.

In my case, I change a large amount of water and frequently. I have it set so the water in the aquarium used for reproduction is automatically changed, little by little, three times a day. The total amount of water changed in one day corresponds to 45% of the entire volume, considering that there is 100 liters in one aquarium. A slight fluctuation in water temperature will be noticed when changing large amounts of water like this, but this can trigger the parent fish to spawn.

It's very difficult to keep extra water for replacement when you have many aquaria, but it is also dreadful to have the water quality decreased by food such as beefheart. Therefore, to be able to maintain good water quality, a continuous exchange of water in large amounts is definitely necessary.

FILTRATION

Generally, there is biological filtration, chemical filtration, and physical filtration. Biological filtration is the dissolution of nitrogenous compounds by filter bacteria. Therefore, a basic filter should have a wide superficial area in order to be able to smoothly circulate the water, thus supplying oxygen needed for bacterial growth and to allow this bacteria to acidify polluting agents.

However, in a discus aquarium it is not practical to depend solely on biological filtration to remove polluting agents. Unless the filter system is especially large or the number of fish kept and the amount of food given is small, one filter system alone cannot usually be enough.

Nitrification caused by bacteria is most apt to happen in alkaline water (pH 7.1-7.8) and the more acid the water, the less nitrification will take place. If pH reaches 6.5, nitrification will stop completely. In other words, the most suitable pH in which to keep discus is when the pH is at the level at which nitrification is most likely not to happen.

Tap water in itself is not the best water for the fish because it contains chemicals such as chlorine. This water should be chemically filtered using activated charcoal before or even after it has been added to the aquarium. Organic compounds, carbon dioxide, ammonia, and heavy metals dissolved in the water can be removed by chemical filtration. The surface of the activated

charcoal has many pores, and material is adsorbed by them. Activated charcoal can be used in many kinds of filters. However, when its pores become filled with adsorbed material, it will lose its effectiveness. Therefore, it must be changed or reactivated. Usually it is changed because reactivation is difficult.

Also, if there is much solid material in the water, this can clog the pores of the activated charcoal. Therefore, it is best to physically filter the water to remove such solid material before running it through the activated charcoal.

The period of effectiveness of the activated charcoal varies with the size of the aquarium and degree of water pollution. To give you an idea, you may use one gram of activated charcoal to one liter of water, but when doing this try to exchange the activated charcoal as soon as possible.

When running water through the activated charcoal before it is poured into the aquarium, use a filter powerful enough to circulate the water at least once in a period of one hour. When doing this, use at least 5 g of activated charcoal to 1 liter of water. The water should be in good condition in 10-12 hours. If the water may contain parasites, set up an ultraviolet sterilizer.

Ammonium ions dissolved in the water can be removed with zeolite. Use this the same way as the activated charcoal. When it begins to lose its effectiveness, soak it in saturated salt water overnight and rinse it with fresh water before using it. Be careful—if you keep using it without doing this, it may start releasing the ammonia components it had absorbed.

To remove nitrates, there is a synthetic resin from Germany (sold as MP500A). This resin is of a reddish brown color and of cylindrical shape, and it can absorb 20 g of nitrate per liter of resin.

CONSIDERING THE FISH'S FOOD
NECESSARY NOURISHMENT

The essential condition of fish food is the same as of terrestrial animals. It should contain proteins, carbohydrates, fats, minerals, and vitamins. A great deal of research has been conducted on food for commercially edible fishes (such as carp and salmon), but the precautions to be taken are the same for aquarium fishes.

Proteins are the main components of the fish's structure and cells. To ensure growth in the fish, it is said that its food must contain at least 30-36% protein. There are two facts to consider when choosing the source of protein.

First, there are ten different kinds of amino acids the fish is not able to synthesize internally and therefore are needed from an outside source. Second, not all protein is digested and absorbed in the same manner. In general, protein found in the aquatic animal groups is high in quality as food, and the protein found in phytoplankton is also well absorbed.

Energy necessary for metabolism is obtained by food combustion. This is similar to burning fuel to run a car, but the burning process inside an animal's body is more complicated. The heat produced by combustion of fuel is read in calories (a unit used to express the amount of heat necessary to increase by 1°C the temperature of 1 g of distilled water). The heat amount of the three main food groups is shown in the table.

When there is enough carbohydrate, many sorts of energy can be obtained from it, but when there isn't enough, protein and fats will be utilized. Of course, the amount of energy needed differs with the fish's activity level and age.

Table 2. Heat (caloric) values of principal foods.

FOOD	HEAT (Kcal., 1 Kcal. = 1000 cal.)
Carbohydrate	4.1
Fat	9.3
Protein	5.5

(In the case of land animals, urea and other substances resulting from protein burning are not burnable. Therefore, the heat decreases to 4.1.)

Fat is essential to fishes, but the type of fatty acid needed differs with the fish.

The amount of vitamins needed is very small, but essential for growth. Vitamins, acting as enzymes and coenzymes, regulate the changes of the body, influencing the function of the cells. There are 13 to 15 kinds of vitamins necessary to the fish, but since some are able to synthesize vitamins in their bodies, not all kinds of fishes need to have many vitamins in their food.

Fishes in their natural environment will not suffer from a vitamin deficiency, but those in captivity, especially those fed only dried foods, tend to suffer from it.

Calcium and phosphorus are the most important minerals. Most of the calcium intake is obtained from water absorbed through the gills, but all phosphorus intake comes from food. Iron, zinc, magnesium, cobalt, and copper are also needed, but only in very small amounts.

PROBLEMS WITH DISCUS FOOD

Wild discus are known to feed on prawns, insects and their larvae, and on small fishes. This means the discus feed mainly on meat. Therefore, I give them the following foods:

-COMBINATION OF BEEFHEART AND SHRIMP

The staple for fish three weeks old until they reach maturity is a 1:1 combination of beefheart and shrimp with vitamins and minerals added to increase the nutritional value. When making the food, I try to use the best available quality at the time. Dice beefheart into small pieces after thoroughly removing all blood vessels and fat. Use edible marine shrimp (freshwater shrimp will have parasites most of the time). Remove the shell and combine with the same amount of diced beefheart in a bowl. Add liquid vitamins and minerals and mix everything well.

I use the latest model food processor to grind and mix the meat. This is better than the former meat processor with a gigantic blade turning rapidly inside the device. Set the processor for 10-15 seconds to make 250 g of beefheart for adult fish; when making this for young fish just process it for a little longer.

Since shrimp can be expensive, try using a substitute and balance the combination. If mixing only about 20% of the amount of beefheart combination, the nutritional value will be the same even if substituted with beef liver. Squid, fish meat, scallops, krill, and/or fish eggs may be used for shrimp substitutes. However, considering the nutritional and processing value (adhesive power is necessary to keep the food together) advantages, try to use shrimp for at least 30% of the combination.

Feed this combination to fish 10 months or older 3 times a day, and 4-6 times a day to fish younger than this. This food is the best to promote growth, but since it tends to lower the quality of the water, give only enough that the fish can eat in about 10 minutes.

-FROZEN BLOODWORMS

Discus, in general, prefer bloodworms. According to research conducted in Israel, bloodworms are not only nutritious, they contain material that stimulates the discus's growth. They also contain chitin, which helps digestion.

Because bloodworms consume everything from organic matter to a variety of chemical substances while underground, there is a possibility they also carry industrial waste and disease-causing parasites in their bodies. Therefore, I don't think live bloodworms should be fed to discus. I feed only frozen bloodworms because any parasites they contain are killed when frozen. Toxic material may still be left, but I have not encountered any problems.

A specially made frozen bloodworm preparation is made as follows. First, give the bloodworms a formalin solution bath for 20 minutes to disinfect them. The formalin solution can be made by diluting 2.5 cc of undiluted formalin solution containing 37% formaldehyde to one liter of water. After this, thoroughly wash the formalin off, put the bloodworms in a plastic container, and keep them at -18°C for at least two weeks. This might not make them 100% safe, but I've never had any problems. Feed adequate amounts of frozen bloodworms 3-4 times a week along with the beefheart and shrimp combination.

-LIVE FOODS

There are different opinions among discus lovers as to whether live foods are necessary or not. In Southeast Asian countries, commercial discus are raised mainly on live food. In Hong Kong and southern China, water fleas and tubificid worms are the main live foods used in the tropical fish industry besides the discus breeders. In Thailand, mosquito larvae are also fed.

In Singapore and Malaysia, where it is prohibited by law to feed mosquito larvae, worms are fed. On the other hand, in Europe frozen beefheart and bloodworms are mainly fed.

Whiteworms, amphipods, and brine shrimp are sometimes fed. Discus were being successfully raised at the largest discus breeding farm in the United States on a combination of beefheart, fish meat or eggs, vitamins, and minerals. All but the young, which were being fed brine shrimp larvae, were fed such combinations.

Dr. Eduard Schmidt-Focke, from Bad-Hamburg, Germany, was the first person to lecture on the importance of live foods. He feeds a variety of live foods such as water fleas, amphipods, water bugs (corixids), and tubificid worms to his own discus. Among these, all except the water fleas are bred in his basement and back yard.

Judging from the color and condition of his fish and also from my own experiences, discus should be fed live foods daily — at least to a certain extent. Although it is possible to keep them only on prepared food combinations, these alone will not allow the discus to be at its best.

However, I am against feeding freshwater animals to discus. The nutritional value and digestive rate cannot be overlooked, but its continued use in regular amounts can lead to diseases. The discus may play the role of intermediate host for parasites and, in the worst cases, great damage will be suffered. These are some of the parasites hosted by freshwater animals:

Water fleas — nematodes (roundworms), trematodes (flukes), tapeworms, acanthocephalans (spiny-headed worms).

Tubificid worms — tapeworms (cestodes)

Amphipods — acanthocephalans (spiny-headed worms)

As a result of feeding foods carrying poisonous things such as bacteria, insecticides, or heavy metals to the discus, they exhibited symptoms of poisoning such as indigestion and accumulation of stomach fluid. If feeding freshwater foods, use only those that come from a clean environment or those that were cultured.

Since in Hong Kong seafood is available year-round, I feed fresh marine shrimp every day by peeling the shells and grinding up the meat. Depending on the season, I purchase crab, shrimp, and lobster eggs at a local market and mix about 10% of this in a shrimp combination. Such eggs, however, are not legally available in some countries like the United States.

Crabs are another favorite of the discus. The meat and internal organs can both be fed, but to take the meat out from a fresh crab takes time and is not very easy.

Besides these, molluscs such as clams, scallops, and squids can also be fed to the discus in the same manner.

Brine shrimp is one of the best live foods possible to cultivate. Feed algae, malted rice, or rice bran, and they should reach the adult stage in about three weeks.

Whiteworms, amphipods, water bugs, and mosquito larvae can

also be cultivated. Among these, the whiteworm is popular with American and European breeders. It also helps induce the discus to reproduce. However, since it can deteriorate the discus fat, do not feed it any more than 2-3 times a week.

SELECTIVE BREEDING METHODS

The richly colored discus we see today is a product of selective breeding. Such beautiful discus are rarely found in the wild. Some with deep blue-green colors, brilliant like a turquoise stone, may be found, but this is a rarity.

A gene mutation occurring during their reproductive stage is the main cause for such individuals born in the wild. However, the mutation is controlled by sheer accident, with one never knowing when this will happen. Based upon this, ways to artificially induce such mutations are being researched. The most common way today is to use X-rays and ultraviolet rays.

Dr. Schmidt-Focke tried the X-ray method on discus to induce mutation. However, his experiments did not produce any interesting results.

THE DIFFICULTY OF SORTING

The selective breeding method we use is another way to artificially create a new variety. The beautiful variety of discus we are hoping to create will have the color and shape we desire. This can be appraised by the phenotype of each individual. From this, we select the individuals with the desired characteristics, and by mating them we will be solidifying the characters that we desire into our discus strains.

However, the difficulty in selective mating is in the fact that the hereditary structure is not so simple that we are able to judge it by phenotype alone. For example, a fish with red eyes has genes that determine that the color of its eyes will be red. However, in most cases genes that determine a particular character exist in many forms. There are genes that will make the color of the eyes gray and there are genes that will cause them to be brown. Such genes are called alleles or allelomorphs. These allelomorphs are combined during mating and, by law of dominance, will show only one character. Therefore, even if two fish with red eyes are mated, all of their young will not necessarily have red eyes.

To add to this, when a particular character is governed by many genes and when there is a great difference in the parental phenotype, the F_1 young will be born having many types. The parents must be carefully selected because we are not able to determine the genetic form of the discus to be born.

When a desired character is governed by a recessive gene, all these genes may be lost depending on how the selection is made.

SELECTIVE MATING PRECAUTIONS

To select the fish with the perfect desired character (and healthy!) from among them all is a task that requires patience and experience, which makes it even more interesting. However, there are some precautions.

One has to create more than one family line when developing strains, no matter what the breed. This is because in most cases, if a genetic problem arises in one line of the family, this may be resolved by mating individuals with the other line.

The other precaution is, because characters governed by recessive genes will not show in the F_1 phenotype, it's important to secure as many F_1 individuals as possible, in order to be able to make the desired selection from the F_2 and F_3.

Among aquarium fishes, the discus is considered to be one of the largest. Therefore, be prepared to provide the large space and plenty of time required to create a new variety.

To find a discus with good quality in the wild is also difficult. Even nowadays, when the methods of capture are many and the means of transportation have advanced, it is hard to say that more good quality discus are captured in the wild now than back in the beginning of the 1960's.

As proof of this, Royal Blue discus (superior quality blue discus), Tefe Green, and Peruvian Green (superior quality green discus) discus are still highly priced.

It is very rare to find a mutated discus with vivid colors among the many thousands captured in the Amazon. This is because in the natural world such individuals are more easily preyed upon by birds or carnivorous fishes in comparison to the brownish discus. Even if such individuals do exist, most will be preyed upon before they reach the age of reproduction and their genes are lost.

Also, in many cases the physical condition of the discus is not very good by the time it reaches the breeder. This is due to injury, stress, and fatigue caused during transportation. Parasites are another cause for alarm. Some that were harmless when the fish was in the wild may become fatal as soon as the fish is put into an aquarium. Most fish will not survive if they are weak.

It will take approximately one year for the wild fish to adjust to the new aquarium life and 2-3 years until they are able to reproduce. The keeping of wild discus will test the breeder's patience.

PROBLEMS OF THE DISCUS ITSELF

Problems that make selective breeding difficult are also found in the discus itself. The first problem is that discus cannot tolerate inbreeding. Dr. Schmidt-Focke is about the only one who has many generations of the same breed, although there are many problems.

When his Red Turquoise entered the third generation of the same line, problems such as the following began to arise: visible decrease in growth rate, therefore taking longer to reach maturity; more susceptibility to diseases; inability to adapt to aquarium life; refusal to care for the eggs; parents eating their eggs; and parents not secreting enough milk.

To avoid such problems, a breeder may mate a wild discus with the one weakened by continuous inbreeding in order to reinforce the line. This is what is referred to as outbreeding, and the breed resulting is usually very strong.

The next problem is the fact that it takes the discus an average of 18 months until the following generation is produced. In the beginning, the female spawns after 8 months and the male reproduces in 10-12 months. However, as the inbreeding continues, it will take longer for the fish to reach maturity, finally taking 18-24 months or even longer if the fish contract any diseases.

Since it takes 18-20 generations until a pure strain is produced by selective breeding, it is said the total time required for this is more than ten years.

As a third problem, the discus is not an easy fish to breed. Because it takes large amounts of medication to treat most of the diseases, the effect of the medicine may make it unable to reproduce. The male, especially, is more sensitive.

The fourth problem is that discus babies only grow on the parents' milk. The discus baby will refuse to feed on other food besides the milk for a few weeks after birth. Also, the parent fish may eat their eggs; the reason for this is not yet clear.

From facts such as these, we cannot deny that part of the success of reproduction is controlled by the parent fish.

As a last problem, pairing the discus depends entirely upon the choice of the fish itself. No matter how hard we may try to match a desired combination, we cannot force them to pair.

After you overcome all these problems one by one, the satisfaction you feel from a successful spawning and the creation of a new breed is incomparable to anything.

SUGGESTED READING

THE ALLURE OF DISCUS
by Dr. H. R. Axelrod and B. Degen
TFH TS-162, 10 x 14", 192 pages,
over 200 photos
The authors, one who has scoured the
Amazon in pursuit of discus, the other a
world-famous discus breeder, have
combined their knowledge to produce this
tribute to the beauty of the discus.

THE ATLAS OF DISCUS OF THE WORLD
by Dr. H. R. Axelrod & B. Degen
TFH TS-164, 10 x 12", 368 pages,
over 350 photos
The combination of photos and hard fact
provided in this book make it one of the
most valuable discus books ever produced.
Includes important information on all
aspects of discus. Especially useful for
distinguishing the many beautiful discus
varieties available.

DISCUS—A REFERENCE BOOK
by B. Degen
TFH TS-163, 8 ½ x 11", 128 pages,
132 photos
An invaluable reference that provides vital
information for anyone keeping discus.
Sections on care, feeding, reproduction,
health, and more.

DISCUS FOR THE PERFECTIONIST
by J. Wattley
TFH TS-167, 9 x 12", 128 pages,
fully illustrated
The man who pioneered discus breeding in
the United States, Jack Wattley, has
authored this book in unique question and
answer format. You can compare and
contrast the knowledge of discus experts
gathered from around the world.

THE DEGEN BOOK OF DISCUS
by B. Degen
TFH TS-134, 8 ½ x 11", 160 pages,
360 photos
All the secrets of success with discus are
here. Bernd Degen loves discus too much
to jeopardize even one by keeping his
knowledge for himself.

DR. SCHMIDT-FOCKE'S DISCUS BOOK
by Dr. E. Schmidt-Focke
TFH TS-135, 9 x 12", 128 pages, 180 photos
A bible from the German "Father of
Discus" Sage advice in heartwarming
anecdotal style.

HANDBOOK OF DISCUS by J. Wattley
TFH H-1070, 8 ½ x 11", 112 pages,
100 photos
Jack Wattley's classic best-seller. Anyone
who doesn't have it, should. Concise
information on the spawning and rearing
of discus fry without their parents by the
man who does it better...

DISCUS, HOW TO BREED THEM
by B. Degen
TFH TS-137, 8 ½ x 11", 160 pages,
100 photos
True facts about discus breeding from the
German master. Special information not
available anywhere else, including such
topics as developing a breeding line, discus
exhibition, technical layout of the discus
room, and more...

DR. CLIFFORD CHAN'S BOOK OF SINGAPORE DISCUS
by C. Chan
TFH TS-170
Dr. Chan has produced a delightful book
full of wonderful techniques developed
and tested in his discus tanks. Cuts through
the confusion usually associated with the
myriad Far Eastern discus varieties. Laden
with photos that make identification of Far
Eastern discus strains easy and fun.
Includes illustrated interviews with all the
major discus breeders in Singapore.

DISCUS HEALTH by D. Untergasser
*Selection, Care, Diet, Diseases &
Treatment for Discus, Angelfish, and
Other Cichlids*
TFH TS-169, 7 x 10", over 400 pages,
fully illustrated
The first book of its kind—devoted to the
health of your discus.

INDEX

Bold means photo or illustration.